Themes from the Scriptures
of the New Testament

By

Thomas Sutton

ISBN: 978-0-7596-5045-9 (sc)
ISBN: 978-0-7596-5044-2 (e)

Print information available on the last page.

This book is printed on acid free paper.

1stBooks – rev. 08/13/01

Table of Contents

About the Book

I wrote this book to be used as an aid. I chose the themes and scriptures. If you think of other scriptures that were left out, add them. After publishing this book, I know I'll find additional scriptures I left out and wish I had included them.

Some of the same verses were used under different themes. God's Word is complex, simple, and can take you down paths that go deep into your spirit. One minister I know refers to studying specific scriptures as "entering the deep end of the pool."

My book is not an attempt to replace the necessity to read and study the scriptures directly from the Bible. This book is just a starting point for you to build your own scriptural reference related to specific themes.

At first, I planned to write this book only for me. I've always had a hard time memorizing lots of scriptures and remembering where to find a scripture relevant to a certain issue. After writing this book, I changed my mind and decided to share this work with others.

After listing a theme, I listed the Books, Chapters, and Verses followed by the actual scriptures. I hope you find this book helpful as you study the Word of God.

Introduction

It was once said, "The Cross wasn't a ladder." No matter what works we do or what laws we follow, we can't force our way into heaven. Like trying to put a square peg into a round hole, we just don't fit. From the beginning when Adam and Eve disobeyed God, sin has separated us from God.

Before the Law of the Ten Commandments was given to Moses, sin existed.

"Later, Cain brought some food from the ground as a gift to God. Abel brought the best parts from some of the first born of his flock. The Lord accepted Abel and his gift, but he did not accept Cain and his gift. So Cain became very angry and felt rejected.

"The Lord asked Cain, 'Why are you angry? Why do you look so unhappy? If you do things well, I will accept you, but if you do not do them well, sin is ready to attack you. Sin wants you, but you must rule over it.'"

Cain attacks his brother Abel and kills him.

"Later, the Lord said to Cain, 'Where is your brother Abel?'

"Cain answered, 'I don't know. Is it my job to take care of my brother?'" In 2001, we are still asking that same question.

Sin became so pervasive that God flooded the earth. Noah and his family (eight people) were the only people God saved. Only a few meant only a few! It wasn't long after the flood that God destroyed Sodom and Gomorrah because of sin. From the beginning, God had a plan that would take away the sins of the world. That plan started with an agreement with Abraham and ended with a new agreement through the death, burial, and resurrection of Jesus Christ.

In the Old Testament, we were guided by God. The Old Testament is the New Testament concealed. Paul writes in Ephesians 3:9-12 "And God gave me the work of telling all people about the plan for his secret, which has been hidden in him since the beginning of time. He is the One who created everything. His purpose was that through the church all the rulers and powers in the heavenly world will now know God's wisdom, which has so many forms. This agrees with the purpose God had since the beginning of time, and he carried out his plan through Christ Jesus our Lord. In Christ we can come before God with freedom and without fear. We can do this through faith in Christ."

The New Testament reveals the Old Testament. In the New Testament, through Jesus, the prophecy of the Old Testament is fulfilled.

The Bible has one theme: human life has meaning in God.

My book starts with two essays. In the first essay, *Why Should You Believe The Bible?*, I make the argument of why you can be certain that the Bible is God's Word. The next essay is titled *Jesus Prophesied*. It includes some of the more than 300 prophecies and references to Christ from the Old Testament written approximately 700 years before Christ.

After the two essays, the themes begin. A theme is stated and followed by New Testament scriptures that are relevant.

Why Should You Believe The Bible? *An Essay*

Paul writes that all Scripture is God-breathed. 2 Timothy 3:16-17 "All Scripture is given by God and is useful for teaching, for showing people what is wrong with their lives, for correcting faults, and for teaching how to live right. Using the Scriptures, the person who serves God will be capable, having all that is needed to do every good work."

Peter writes in 2 Peter 1:19-21 "This makes us more sure about the message the prophets gave. It is good for you to follow closely what they said as you would follow a light shining in a dark place, until the day begins and the morning star rises in your hearts. Most of all, you must understand this: No prophecy in the Scriptures ever comes from the prophet's own interpretation. No prophecy ever came from what a person wanted to say, but people led by the Holy Spirit spoke words from God."

In Exodus 4:11-12 of the Old Testament, God says to Moses, "Then the Lord said to him, 'Who made a person's mouth? And who makes someone deaf or not able to speak? Or who gives a person sight or blindness? It is I, the Lord. Now go! I will help you speak, and I will teach you what to say.'"

Exodus 34:27 "Then the Lord said to Moses, 'Write down these words, because with these words I have made an agreement with you and Israel.'"

Moses wrote the first five books of the Old Testament. Four-hundred twenty times he says that the words he has written are from God. Eighty times Isaiah says, "This is what the Lord says."

In Jeremiah 1:9, Jeremiah writes, "Then the Lord reached out his hand and touched my mouth. He said to me, 'See, I am putting my words in your mouth.'"

Micah 1:1 "During the time that Jotham, Ahaz, and Hezekiah were kings of Judah, the word of the Lord came to Micah, who was from Moresheth. He saw these visions about Samaria and Jerusalem." Throughout Micah he says, "That is what the Lord says," "The Lord says." Amos and Malachi say the same thing... "The Lord said," "The Lord says."

You should believe the Bible because of the fulfillment of prophecy. Seven-hundred years before Christ, the writers and prophets of the Old Testament told of the New Agreement through the Savior Jesus Christ. Jeremiah 31: 31-32. "Look, the time is coming," says the Lord,

"when I will make a new agreement
with the people of Israel
and the people of Judah.
It will not be like the agreement
I made with their ancestors
when I took them by the hand
to bring them out of Egypt.
I was a husband to them,
but they broke that agreement," says the Lord.

In the New Testament, John writes in 1 John 1:1-4 "We write you now about what has always existed, which we have heard, we have seen with our own eyes, we have looked at, and we have touched with our hands. We write to you about the Word that gives life. He who gives life was shown to us. We saw him and can give proof about it. And now we announce to you that he has life that continues forever. He was with God the Father and was shown to us. We announce to you what we have seen and heard, because we want you also to have fellowship with us. Our fellowship is with God the Father and with his Son, Jesus Christ. We write this to you so you can be full of joy with us."

Jesus and the writers of the New Testament quote and give references to the Old Testament numerous times. In Matthew 5:17-20, Jesus says, "Don't think that I have come to destroy the law of Moses or the teaching of the prophets. I have not come to destroy them but to bring about what they said. I tell you the truth, nothing will disappear from the law until heaven and earth are gone. Not even the smallest letter or the smallest part of a letter will be lost until everything has happened. Whoever refuses to obey any command and teaches other people not to obey that command will be the least important in the kingdom of heaven. But whoever obeys the commands and teaches other people to obey them will be great in the kingdom of heaven. I tell you that if you are no more obedient than the teachers of the law and the Pharisees, you will never enter the kingdom of heaven." Jesus quotes Hosea 6:6, Isaiah 6:9-10; 29:13; 13:10; 34:4, Psalms 118:22-23,26;110:1, Zechariah 13:7.

Another reason to believe in The Bible is because of how it's written; i.e. the **brevity** and **omission** of scriptures and the **impartiality** and **unity** of the scriptures. In Genesis, there are 2500 years in 50 chapters. The Creation story is written in 27 verses. In Mark of the New Testament, the life of Christ is told in 16 chapters. The history of the Church is found in 28 chapters of Acts.

In the four biographies of Christ, there is no mention of Jesus' appearance and no mention about the other days of Jesus' life. How did Paul die?

The writers told both the good and bad. Noah built an Ark and later he got drunk. Paul persecuted Christians. King David broke most of the Ten Commandments, including murder.

There is unity in the 66 books of the Bible. The Bible focuses on Jesus. In the Old Testament, we were guided by God. The Old Testament is the New Testament concealed. The New Testament reveals the Old Testament. In the New Testament, through Jesus, the prophecy of the Old Testament is fulfilled. **The Bible has one theme: Human life has meaning in God.**

Other Evidence

In 1947, the Dead Sea Scrolls were discovered in caves near Khirbat. They contained two of the oldest known copies of the Book of Isaiah. They also contained fragments of every book in the Old Testament except Esther. When compared to other writings, no differences were found. Paleographic evidence indicates that most of the Dead Sea Scrolls were written between approximately 200 BC and 68 AD.

The numerous copies of the New Testament give it reliability. There are approximately 5000 manuscripts from original Greek texts. The New Testament was first written in 100 AD. The earliest manuscript was written only 250 years later. When you compare this to other writings like Plato, (whose earliest manuscripts were written 900 to 1200 years later), the New Testament is the most reliable of all historical manuscripts.

Other accounts of Jesus and his crucifixion can be found in the book of Josephus, who lived during Christ time. Thalleus and Pallegus also wrote about Jesus. The life of Jesus can be pieced together from these writers alone, without even using The Bible.

Archeology confirms the Bible. Archeologists are constantly finding and digging up cities that are mentioned in The Bible.

History documents the Roman Empire and the Christian movement; i.e. Christians were being fed to the lions as sport.

If you still don't believe in the Bible, you should ask yourself, "Why?"

Jesus Prophesied *An Essay*

Psalm 132:11 The Lord made a promise to David,
    a sure promise that he will not take back.
He promised, "I will make one of your descendants
    rule as king after you."
God promised David that he would make a descendant from his family rule as king.

Isaiah 11:10 At that time the new king from the family of Jesse will stand as a banner for all peoples. The nations will come together around him, and the place where he lives will be filled with glory.
The new king who Isaiah is talking about is Jesus. In Ruth 4:22 Jesse was the father of David, king of Israel. Jesus was from their family.

Psalm 16:8-11 I keep the Lord before me always.
    Because he is close by my side,
    I will not be hurt.
So I rejoice and am glad.
    Even my body has hope,
because you will not leave me in the grave.
    You will not let your holy one rot.
You will teach me how to live a holy life.
    Being with you will fill me with joy;
    at your right hand I will find pleasure forever.
David is talking about the Christ rising from the dead.

Isaiah 25:8...he will destroy death forever.
The Lord God will wipe away every tear
    from every face.
He will take away the shame of his people from
    the earth.
The Lord has spoken.

Hosea 13:14 Will I save them from the place of the dead?
    Will I rescue them from death?
Where is your sickness, death?
    Where is your pain, place of death?
    I will show them no mercy.
Isaiah and Hosea are talking about how death is destroyed forever in Christ.

Micah 5:2 "But you, Bethlehem Ephrathah,
though you are too small to be among the army
    groups from Judah,
from you will come one who will rule Israel for me.
    He comes from very old times,
    from days long ago."

Isaiah 59:20-21 "Then a savior will come to Jerusalem
and to the people of Jacob who have
    turned from sin,"
says the Lord.
The Lord says, "This is my agreement with these people: My Spirit and my
words that I give you will never leave you or your children or your
grandchildren, now and forever."

Isaiah 27:9 This is how Israel's guilt will be forgiven;
    this is how its sins will be taken away:
Israel will crush the rocks of the altar to dust,
    and no statues or altars will be left standing for the Asherah idols.

Isaiah 7:14-15 "The Lord himself will give you a sign: The virgin will be
pregnant. She will have a son, and she will name him Immanuel. He will be
eating milk curds and honey when he learns to reject what is evil and to choose
what is good."
*A man named Joseph, a descendent of David, was engaged to be married to
a virgin named Mary. An angel said to Mary that the Lord had blessed her and
was with her. The angel informed her that she would become pregnant by the
power of the Holy Spirit and give birth to a son. Jesus was born in Bethlehem.
An angel told Mary and Joseph to name him Jesus, which means salvation. He
would be called the Son of the Most High, the Son of God. He would be Holy,
and the Lord would give him the throne of King David to rule over the people
with a Kingdom that would never end. He would save people from their sins.*

Jeremiah 31:15 This is what the Lord says:
"A voice was heard in Ramah
    of painful crying and deep sadness:
Rachel crying for her children.
    She refused to be comforted,
    because her children are dead!"

Herod gave an order to kill all the baby boys who were two-years old or younger in Bethlehem and in all the surrounding areas. This was because of what he learned from the wise men.

Isaiah 8:18 I am here, and with me are the children the Lord has given me. We are signs and proofs for the people of Israel from the Lord All-powerful, who lives on Mount Zion.

Psalms 97:7 Those who worship idols should be ashamed;
    they brag about their gods.
    All the gods should worship the Lord.

Psalms 2:7 Now I will tell you what the Lord has declared:
He said to me, "You are my son.
    Today I have become your Father."

2 Samuel 7:14 "I will be his Father, and he will be my Son."

Psalms 45:6-7 "God, your throne will last forever and ever.
    You will rule your kingdom with fairness.
You love right and hate evil,
    so God has chosen you from among your friends;
    he has set you apart with much joy.

Psalm 102:25-27 In the beginning you made the earth,
    and your hands made the skies.
They will be destroyed, but you will remain.
    They will all wear out like clothes.
And, like clothes you will change them.
    And throw them away.
But you never change,
    and your life will never end.

Psalm 110:1 The Lord said to my Lord,
"Sit by me at my right side
    until I put your enemies under your control."

Psalms 40:6-8 You do not want sacrifices and offerings.
    But you have made a hole in my ear
    to show that my body and life are yours.
You do not ask for burnt offerings
    and sacrifices to take away sins.

Then I said, "Look, I have come.
    It is written about me in the book.
My God, I want to do what you want.
    Your teachings are in my heart."

Jeremiah 31: 31-34 "Look, the time is coming," says the Lord,
    "when I will make a new agreement
with the people of Israel
    and the people of Judah.
It will not be like the agreement
    I made with their ancestors
when I took them by the hand
    to bring them out of Egypt.
I was a husband to them,
    but they broke that agreement," says the Lord.
"This is the agreement I will make
    with them at that time,"
    says the Lord:
"I will put my teachings in their minds
    and write them on their hearts.
I will be their God,
    and they will be my people.
People will no longer have to teach their neighbors
    and relatives
    to know the Lord,
because all people will know me,
    from the least to the most important,"
    says the Lord.
"I will forgive them for the wicked things they did,
    and I will not remember their sins anymore."

God brings people to Jesus. The signs and proofs for the people of Israel are Jesus and His children. Jesus is God's Son, and His throne will last forever and ever. Under the new agreement, sin is no longer taken away with burnt offerings and sacrifices. The teachings of the new agreement are in their minds and written on their hearts. Jesus will take away their sins.

Isaiah 40:3-5 This is the voice of one who calls out:
"Prepare in the desert
    the way for the Lord.
Make a straight road in the dry lands
    for our God.
Every valley should be raised up,

and every mountain and hill should be made flat.
The rough ground should be made level,
    and the rugged ground should be made smooth.
Then the glory of the Lord will be shown,
    and all people together will see it.
The Lord himself said these things."

Malachi 3:1 The Lord All-Powerful says, "I will send my messenger, who will prepare the way for me. Suddenly, the Lord you are looking for will come to his Temple; the messenger of the agreement, whom you want, will come."
Isaiah and Malachi are talking about John the Baptist, who prepares for the way of the Lord.

Psalm 91:11-12 He put his angels in charge of you
    to watch over you wherever you go.
They will catch you in their hands
    so that you will not hit your foot on a rock.
The devil quotes this scripture to tempt Jesus to jump from a high place to test the Lord.

Isaiah 9:1-2 But suddenly there will be no more gloom for the land that suffered. In the past God made the lands of Zebulun and Naphtali hang their heads in shame, but in the future those lands will be made great. They will stretch from the road along the Mediterranean Sea to the land beyond the Jordan River and north to Galilee, the land of people who are not Israelites.

Before those people lived in darkness,
    but now they have seen a great light.
They lived in a dark land,
    but a light has shined on them.
Jesus leaves Nazareth and lives in Capernaum, a town near Lake Galilee in an area near Zebulun and Naphtali.

Isaiah 53:1-6 Who would have believed what we heard?
Who saw the Lord's power in this?
He grew up like a small plant before the Lord,
    like a root growing in a dry land.
He had no special beauty or form to make us notice him;
    there was nothing in his appearance to make us desire him.
He was hated and rejected by people.
    He had much pain and suffering.
People would not even look at him.
    He was hated, and we didn't even notice him.

But he took our suffering on him
    and felt our pain for us.
We saw his suffering
    and thought God was punishing him.
But he was wounded for the wrong we did;
    he was crushed for the evil we did.
The punishment, which made us well, was given to him,
    and we are healed because of his wounds.
We all have wandered away like sheep;
    each of us has gone his own way.
But he Lord has put on him the punishment
    for all the evil we have done.

The Jews are expecting the Christ to rule over a physical, earthly kingdom, like king David did. Jesus was hated and rejected by the people. He suffered and felt our pain on the Cross. The punishment that freed us from sin was given to him.

Isaiah 56:7 "I will bring these people to my holy mountain
    and give them joy in my house of prayer.
The offerings and sacrifices
    they place on my altar will please me,
because my Temple will be called
    a house for prayer for people from all nations."

Jeremiah 7:11 This place where I have chosen to be worshiped is nothing more to you than a hideout for robbers. I have been watching you, says the Lord.

Psalm 69:9 My strong love for your Temple completely controls me.
    When people insult you, it hurts me.

Jesus goes into the Temple and throws out all the people who were buying and selling there. He turned over the tables of those who were exchanging different kinds of money, and he upset the benches of those who were selling doves. Jesus said to all the people who were there, "It is written in the Scriptures, 'My Temple will be called a house for prayer.' But you are changing it into a 'hideout for robbers.'"

Jesus said to those who were selling pigeons, "Take these things out of here! Don't make my Father's house a place for buying and selling!" When this happened, the followers remembered what was written in the Scriptures: "My strong love for your Temple completely controls me."

Isaiah 61:1 The Lord God has put his Spirit in me,
because the Lord has appointed me to tell
    the good news to the poor.
He has sent me to comfort those whose hearts are broken,
to tell the captives they are free,
    and to tell the prisoners they are released.

Isaiah 58:6 "I will tell you the kind of special day I want:
Free the people you have put in prison unfairly
    and undo their chains.
Free those to whom you are unfair
    and stop their hard labor."

Isaiah 61:2 He has sent me to announce the time when the
    Lord will show his kindness
and the time when our God will punish
    evil people.
He has sent me to comfort all those who are sad.
Jesus stands and reads the previous verses from the book of Isaiah. Jesus closes the book, gives it back to the assistant, and sits down. Everyone in the synagogue was watching Jesus closely. Jesus said to them, "While you heard these words just now, they were coming true."

Isaiah 54:13 All your children will be taught by the Lord,
    And they will have much peace.
Jesus said, "Stop complaining to each other. The Father is the One who sent me. No one can come to me unless the Father draws him to me, and I will raise that person up on the last day. It is written in the prophets, 'They will all be taught by God.'"

Micah 7:6 A son will not honor his father,
    a daughter will turn against her mother,
and a daughter-in-law will be against her
    mother-in-law;
    a person's enemies will be members of
    his own family.
Jesus didn't come to bring peace but a sword.

Isaiah 42:1-4 "Here is my servant, the one I support.
He is the one I chose, and I am pleased
    with him.
I have put my Spirit upon him,

and he will bring justice to all nations.
He will not cry out or yell
 or speak loudly in the streets.
He will not break a crushed blade of grass
 or put out even a weak flame.
He will truly bring justice;
 he will not lose hope or give up
until he brings justice to he world.
 And people far away will trust his teachings."

Psalms 2:7-12 Now I tell you what the Lord has declared:
He said to me, "You are my son.
 Today I have become your father.
If you ask me, I will give you the nations;
 all the people on earth will be yours.
You will rule over them with an iron rod.
 You will break them into pieces like pottery."

So, kings, be wise;
 rulers, learn this lesson.
Obey the Lord with great fear.
 Be happy, but tremble.
Show that you are loyal to his son,
 or you will be destroyed by his anger,
because he can quickly become angry.
 But happy are those who trust him for protection.
The previous scriptures are about God's son and chosen servant, Jesus.

Isaiah 6:9-10 Then the Lord said, "Go and tell this to the people:
 'You will listen and listen, but you will not understand.
 You will look and look, but you will not learn.'
Make the minds of these people dumb.
 Shut their ears. Cover their eyes.
Otherwise, they might really understand
 what they see with their eyes
 and hear with their ears.
They might really understand in their minds
 and come back to me and be healed."

Psalms 78:2 I will speak using stories;
 I will tell secret things from long ago.
Jesus used stories to teach.

Isaiah 53:1 Who would have believed what we heard?
Who saw the Lord's power in this?

Isaiah 29:14 "So I will continue to amaze these people
by doing more and more miracles.
Their wise men will lose their wisdom;
their wise men will not be able to understand."
Even though Jesus had done many miracles in front of the people, some people didn't believe in Jesus.

Isaiah 62:11 The Lord is speaking
to all the faraway lands:
"Tell the people of Jerusalem,
'Look, your Savior is coming.
He is bringing your reward to you;
he is bringing his payment with him.'"

Zechariah 9:9 Rejoice greatly, people of Jerusalem!
Shout for joy, people of Jerusalem!
Your king is coming to you.
He does what is right, and he saves.
He is gentle and riding on a donkey,
on the colt of a donkey.

Psalms 118:25-26 Please, Lord, save us;
please, Lord, give us success.
God bless the one who comes in the name of
the Lord.
We bless all of you from the Temple of the Lord.
Jesus the Savior enters Jerusalem as a king riding on a donkey.

Isaiah 8:14-15 "Then he will be a place of safety for you.
But for the two families of Israel,
he will be like a stone that causes people to stumble,
like a rock that makes them fall.
He will be like a trap for the people of Jerusalem,
and he will catch them in his trap.
Many people will fall over this rock.
They will fall and be broken;
they will be trapped and caught."

Isaiah 28:16 Because of these things, this is what the Lord God says;
"I will put a stone in the ground in Jerusalem,
>a tested stone.

Everything will be built on this important and precious rock.
>Anyone who trusts in it will never be disappointed.

Psalms 118:22-23 The stone that the builders rejected
>became the cornerstone.

The Lord did this,
>and it is wonderful to us.

Jesus is the rock that makes them fall—the tested stone that the builders rejected.

Psalms 110: 1 The Lord said to my Lord,
"Sit by me at my right side
until I put your enemies under your control."
The Pharisees think the Christ is the Son of David. Jesus says, "David calls the Christ 'Lord' so how can the Christ be his son?"

Psalms 41:9 My best and truest friend, who ate at my table,
>has even turned against me.

Jesus says to his apostles, "I am not talking about all of you. I know those I have chosen. But this is to bring about what the Scripture said: 'The man who ate at my table has turned against me.' I am telling you this now before it happens so that when it happens, you will believe that I am he. I tell you the truth, whoever accepts anyone I send also accepts me. And whoever accepts me also accepts the One who sent me."

Psalms 35:19 Do not let my enemies laugh at me;
>they hate me for no reason.

Do not let them make fun of me;
>they have no cause to hate me.

Psalm 69:4 There are more people who hate me for no reason
>than hairs on my head;

powerful enemies want to destroy me
>for no reason.

They make me pay back
>what I did not steal.

Psalms 2:1-2 Why are the nations so angry?
Why are the people making useless plans?
The kings of the earth prepare to fight,

and their leaders make plans together
against the Lord
and his appointed one.

Jesus says, "I did works among them that no one else has ever done. If I had not done these works, they would not be guilty of sin. But now they have seen what I have done, and yet they have hated both me and my Father. But this happened so that what is written in their law would be true: 'They hated me for no reason.'"

Zechariah 11:12-13 Then I said, "If you want to pay me, pay me. If not, then don't." So they paid me thirty pieces of silver.

The Lord said to me, "Throw the money to the potter." That is how little they thought I was worth. So I took the thirty pieces of silver and threw them to the potter in the Temple of the Lord.

Jesus was betrayed by Judas for thirty pieces of silver.

Zechariah 13:7 "Sword, hit the shepherd.
Attack the man who is my friend,"
says the Lord All-Powerful.
"Kill the shepherd,
and the sheep will scatter,
and I will punish the little ones."

Isaiah 53:12 For this reason I will make him a great man among people,
and he will share in all things with those who are strong.
He willingly gave his life
and was treated like a criminal.
But he carried away the sins of many people
and asked forgiveness for those who sinned."

Isaiah 53:7-8 He was beaten down and punished,
but he didn't say a word.
He was like a lamb being led to be killed.
He was quiet, as a sheep is quiet while its wool is being cut;
he never opened his mouth.
Men took him away roughly and unfairly.
He died without children to continue his family.
He was put to death;
he was punished for the sins of my people.
Psalms 22:17-18 I can count all my bones;
people look and stare at me.
They divided my clothes among them,

and they threw lots for my clothing.

Psalms 22:15 My strength has dried up like a clay pot,
and my tongue sticks to the top of my mouth.
You laid me in the dust of death.

Psalm 69:21 They put poison in my food
and gave me vinegar to drink.

Psalms 34:20 He will protect their very bones;
not one of them will be broken.

Zechariah 12:10 "I will pour out on David's family and the people in Jerusalem a spirit of kindness and mercy. They will look at me, the one they have stabbed, and they will cry like someone crying over the death of an only child. They will be as sad as someone who has lost a firstborn son.

Jesus was treated like a criminal, beaten and crucified, but he didn't say a word. He was like a lamb being led to be killed. Not one bone in his body was broken. They divided his clothes and threw lots for his clothing.

These are just a few of the 300 prophecies and references to Christ from the Old Testament written approximately 700 years before Christ.

Salvation With Baptism: Baptism To Wash Your Sins Away

Matthew 3:13-17 At that time Jesus came from Galilee to the Jordan River and wanted John to baptize him. But John tried to stop him, saying, "Why do you come to me to be baptized? I need to be baptized by you!"

Jesus answered, "Let it be this way for now. We should do all things that are God's will." So John agreed to baptize Jesus.

As soon as Jesus was baptized, he came up out of the water. Then heaven opened, and he saw God's Spirit coming down on him like a dove. And a voice from heaven said, "This is my Son, whom I love, and I am very pleased with him."

Mark 1:9-11 Same as above with variations.
Luke 3:21-22 Same as above with variations.

Matthew 28:18-20 Then Jesus came to them and said, "All power in heaven and on earth is given to me. So go and make followers of all people in the world. Baptize them in the name of the Father and the Son and the Holy Spirit. Teach them to obey everything that I have taught you, and I will be with you always, even until the end of this age."

Mark 16:15-16 Jesus said to his followers, "Go everywhere in the world, and tell the Good News to everyone. Anyone who believes and is baptized will be saved, but anyone who does not believe will be punished."

Luke 7:29-30 (When the people, including the tax collectors, heard this, they all agreed that God's teaching was good, because they had been baptized by John. But the Pharisees and experts on the law refused to accept God's plan for themselves; they did not let John baptize them.)

John 3:5 But Jesus answered, "I tell you the truth, unless one is born from water and the Spirit, he cannot enter God's kingdom."

John 4:1-2 The Pharisees heard that Jesus was making and baptizing more followers than John, although Jesus himself did not baptize people, but his followers did.

Acts 2:38 Peter said to them, "Change your hearts and lives and be baptized, each one of you, in the name of Jesus Christ for the forgiveness of your sins. And you will receive the gift of the Holy Spirit. This promise is for you, for your children, and for all who are far away. It is for everyone the Lord our God calls to himself."

Acts 2:41 Then those people who accepted what Peter said were baptized. About three thousand people were added to the number of believers that day.

Acts 8:12-13 But when Philip told them the Good News about the kingdom of God and the power of Jesus Christ, men and women believed Philip and were baptized. Simon himself believed, and after he was baptized, he stayed very close to Philip. When he saw the miracles and the powerful things Philip did, Simon was amazed.

Acts 8:36-38 (Philip teaches an Ethiopian) While they were traveling down the road, they came to some water. The officer said, "Look, here is water. What is stopping me from being baptized?" Then the officer commanded the chariot to stop. Both Philip and the officer went down into the water, and Philip baptized him.

Acts 9:18 (Paul is baptized) Immediately, something that looked like fish scales fell from Saul's eyes, and he was able to see again! Then Saul got up and was baptized.

Acts 10:47-48 "Can anyone keep these people from being baptized with water? They have received the Holy Spirit just as we did!" So Peter ordered that they be baptized in the name of Jesus Christ. Then they asked Peter to stay with them for a few days.

Acts 16:29-33 The jailer told someone to bring a light. Then he ran inside and, shaking with fear, fell down before Paul and Silas. He brought them outside and said, "Men, what must I do to be saved?"
They said to him, "Believe in the Lord Jesus and you will be saved—you and all the people in your house." So Paul and Silas told the message of the Lord to the jailer and all the people in his house. At that hour of the night the jailer took Paul and Silas and washed their wounds. Then he and all his people were baptized immediately.

Acts 16:15 (Lydia becomes a Christian) She and all the people in her house were baptized....

Acts 18:8 Crispus was the leader of that synagogue, and he and all the people living in his house believed in the Lord. Many others in Corinth also listened to Paul and believed and were baptized.

Acts 19:1-6 (Paul in Ephesus) While Apollos was in Corinth, Paul was visiting some places on the way to Ephesus. There he found some followers and asked them, "Did you receive the Holy Spirit when you believed?"

They said, "We have never even heard of a Holy Spirit."

So he asked, "What kind of baptism did you have?"

They said, "It was the baptism that John taught."

Paul said, "John's baptism was a baptism of changed hearts and lives. He told people to believe in the one who would come after him, and that one is Jesus."

When they heard this, they were baptized in the name of the Lord Jesus. Then Paul laid his hands on them, and the Holy Spirit came upon them. They began speaking different languages and prophesying.

Acts 22:16 "Now, why wait any longer? Get up, be baptized, and wash your sins away, trusting in him to save you."

Romans 6:3-4 Did you forget that all of us became part of Christ when we were baptized? We shared his death in our baptism. When we were baptized, we were buried with Christ and shared his death. So, just as Christ was raised from the dead by the wonderful power of the Father, we also can live a new life.

I Corinthians 6:11 In the past, some of you were like that, but you were washed clean. You were made holy, and you were made right with God in the name of the Lord Jesus Christ and in the Spirit of our God.

I Corinthians 12:13 Some of us are Jews, and some are Geeks. Some of us are slaves, and some are free. But we were all baptized into one body through one Spirit. And we were all made to share in the one Spirit.

I Corinthians 15:29 If the dead are never raised, what will people do who are being baptized for the dead? If the dead are not raised at all, why are people being baptized for them?

Galatians 3:26-27 You were all baptized into Christ, and so you were all clothed with Christ. This means that you are all children of God through faith in Christ Jesus.

Ephesians 4:5 There is one Lord, one faith, one baptism.

Colossians 2:11-15 Also in Christ you had a different kind of circumcision, a circumcision not done by hands. It was through Christ's circumcision, that is, his death, that you were made free from the power of your sinful self. When you were baptized, you were buried with Christ, and you were raised up with him through your faith in God's power that was shown when he raised Christ from the dead. When you were spiritually dead because of your sins and because you were not free from the power of your sinful self, God made you alive with Christ, and he forgave all our sins. He canceled the debt, which listed all the rules we failed to follow. He took away that record with its rules and nailed it to the cross. God stripped the spiritual rulers and powers of their authority. With the cross, he won the victory and showed the world that they were powerless.

Colossians 2:20-23 Since you died with Christ and were made free from the ruling spirits of the world, why do you act as if you still belong to this world by following rules like these: "Don't eat this," "Don't taste that," "Don't even touch that thing"? These rules refer to earthy things that are gone as soon as they are used. They are only man-made commands and teachings. They seem to be wise, but they are only part of a man-made religion. They make people pretend not to be proud and make them punish their bodies, but they do not really control the evil desires of the sinful self.

Titus 3:4-5...He saved us through the washing that made us new people through the Holy Spirit.

Hebrews 6:1-3 So let us go on to grown-up teaching. Let us not go back over the beginning lessons we learned about Christ. We should not again start teaching about faith in God and about turning away from those acts that lead to death. We should not return to the teaching about baptisms, about laying on of hands, about the raising of the dead and eternal judgment. And we will go on to grown-up teaching if God allows.

Hebrews 10:22 Let us come near to God with a sincere heart and a sure faith, because we have been made free from a guilty conscience, and our bodies have been washed with pure water.

I Peter 3:21 And that water is like baptism that now saves you—not the washing of dirt from the body, but the promise made to God from a good conscience. And this is because Jesus Christ was raised from the dead.

I John 5:6-7 Jesus Christ is the One who came by water and blood. He did not come by water only, but by water and blood. And the Spirit says that this is true, because the Spirit is the truth. So there are three witnesses that tell us about Jesus: the Spirit, the water, and the blood; and these three witnesses agree.

Note: *Baptism is not for merit. It is not 'a works.' It cleanses us of our sins. It is the essence of our obedience to God. When we are baptized, we are buried with Christ and raised up with him through our faith in God's power. Baptism connects us to the Cross of Jesus. We are saved by Grace through believing in Jesus Christ.*

Salvation Without Baptism?

Acts 10:43 "All the prophets say it is true that all who believe in Jesus will be forgiven of their sins through Jesus' name."

Acts 15:11 "But we believe that we and they too will be saved by the grace of the Lord Jesus."

Romans 3:22-26 God makes people right with himself through their faith in Jesus Christ. This is true for all who believe in Christ, because all people are the same: All have sinned and are not good enough for God's glory, and all need to be made right with God by his grace, which is a free gift. They need to be made free from sin through Jesus Christ. God gave him as a way to forgive sin through faith in the blood of Jesus' death. This showed that God always does what is right and fair, as in the past when he was patient and did not punish people for their sins. And God gave Jesus to show today that he does what is right. God did this so he could judge rightly and so he could make right any person who has faith in Jesus.

Romans 3:27-28 So do we have a reason to brag about ourselves? No! And why not? It is the way of faith that stops all bragging, not the way of trying to obey the law. A person is made right with God through faith, not through obeying the law.

Romans 4:9-12 Is this blessing only for those who are circumcised or also for those who are not circumcised? We have already said that God accepted Abraham's faith and that faith made him right with God. So how did this happen? Did God accept Abraham before or after he was circumcised? It was before his circumcision. Abraham was circumcised to show that he was right with God through faith before he was circumcised. So Abraham is the father of all those who believe but are not circumcised; he is the father of all believers who are accepted as being right with God. And Abraham is also the father of those who have been circumcised and who live following the faith that our father Abraham had before he was circumcised.

Colossians 2:11-12 Also in Christ you had a different king of circumcision, a circumcision not done by hands. It was through Christ's circumcision, that is, his death, that you were made free from the power of your sinful self. When you were baptized, you were buried with Christ, and you were raised up with him through your faith in God's power that was shown when he raised Christ from the dead. *(Case for baptism)*

Romans 5:1-3 Since we have been made right with God by our faith, we have peace with God. This happened through our Lord Jesus Christ, who has brought us into the blessing of God's grace that we now enjoy. And we are happy because of the hope we have of sharing God's glory.

Romans 10:9-13 If you use your mouth to say, "Jesus is Lord," and if you believe in your heart that God raised Jesus from the dead, you will be saved. We believe with our hearts, and so we are made right with God. And we use our mouths to say that we believe, and so we are saved. As the Scripture says, "Anyone who trusts in him will never be disappointed." That Scripture says, "anyone" because there is no difference between those who are Jews and those who are not. The same Lord is the Lord of all and gives many blessings to all who trust in him, as the Scripture says, "Anyone who calls on the Lord will be saved."

Ephesians 2:8-10 I mean that you have been saved by grace through believing. You did not save yourselves; it was a gift from God. It was not the result of your own efforts, so you cannot brag about it. God has made us what we are. In Christ Jesus, God made us to do good works, which God planned in advance for us to live our lives doing.

2 Thessalonians 2:13-14 Brothers and sisters, whom the Lord loves, God chose you from the beginning to be saved. So we must always thank God for you. You are saved by the Spirit that makes you holy and by your faith in the truth. God used the Good News that we preached to call you to be saved so you can share in the glory of our Lord Jesus Christ.

Galatians 3:1-5 You people in Galatia were told very clearly about the death of Jesus Christ on the cross. But you were foolish; you let someone trick you. Tell me this one thing: How did you receive the Holy Spirit? Did you receive the Spirit by following the law? No, you received the Spirit because you heard the Good News and believed it. You began your life in Christ by the Spirit. Now are you trying to make it complete by your own power? That is foolish. Were all your experiences wasted? I hope not! Does God give you the Spirit and work miracles among you because you follow the Law? No, he does these things because you heard the Good News and believed it.

Jesus Has Power And Authority Over Everything To Forgive Sins, Judge, And Save People

Mark 2:10-12 "But I will prove to you that the Son of Man has authority on earth to forgive sins." So Jesus said to the paralyzed man, "I tell you, stand up, take your mat, and go home." Immediately the paralyzed man stood up, took his mat, and walked out while everyone was watching him.
Luke 5:21-25 Same as above with variations.

Mark 2:27-28 Then Jesus said to the Pharisees, "The Sabbath day was made to help people; they were not made to be ruled by the Sabbath day. So then, the Son of Man is Lord even of the Sabbath day."

Luke 6:5 Then Jesus said to the Pharisees, "The Son of Man is Lord of the Sabbath day."

Matthew 28:18-20 Then Jesus came to them and said, "All power in heaven and on earth is given to me. So go and make followers of all people in the world. Baptize them in the name of the Father and the Son and the Holy Spirit. Teach them to obey everything that I have taught you, and I will be with you always, even until the end of this age."

John 3:34-36 "The One whom God sent speaks the words of God, because God gives him the Spirit fully. The Father loves the Son and has given him power over everything. Those who believe in the Son have eternal life, but those who do not obey the Son will never have life. God's anger stays on them."

John 5:22-23 In fact, the Father judges no one, but he has given the Son power to do all the judging so that all people will honor the Son as much as they honor the Father. Anyone who does not honor the Son does not honor the Father who sent him.

John 10:30 "The Father and I are one."

John 17:1-5 After Jesus said these things, he looked toward heaven and prayed, "Father, the time has come. Give glory to your Son so that the Son can give glory to you. You gave the Son power over all people so that the Son could give eternal life to all those you gave him. And this is eternal life: that people know you, the only true God, and that they know Jesus Christ, the One you sent. Having finished the work you gave me to do, I brought you glory on earth. And now, Father, give me glory with you; give me the glory I had with you before the world was made."

Acts 4:12 "Jesus is the only One who can save people. His name is the only power in the world that has been given to save people. We must be saved through him."

Acts 10:42-43 "He told us to preach to the people and to tell them that he is the one whom God chose to be the judge of the living and the dead. All the prophets says it is true that all who believe in Jesus will be forgiven of their sins through Jesus' name."

Ephesians 1:9-10 Let us know his secret purpose. This was what God wanted, and he planned to do it through Christ. His goal was to carry out his plan, when the right time came, that all things in heaven and on earth would be joined together in Christ as the head.

Ephesians 1:21-23 God has put Christ over all rulers, authorities, powers, and kings, not only in this world but also in the next. God put everything under his power and made him the head over everything for the church, which is Christ's body. The church is filled with Christ, and Christ fills everything in every way.

Ephesians 2:20-23 You are like a building that was built on the foundation of the apostles and prophets. Christ Jesus himself is the most important stone in that building, and that whole building is joined together in Christ. He makes it grow and become a holy temple in the Lord. And in Christ you, too, are being built together with the Jews into a place where God lives through the Spirit.

1 Peter 3:22 Now Jesus has gone into heaven and is at God's right side ruling over angels, authorities, and powers.

Mark 4:41 The followers were very afraid and asked each other, "Who is this? Even the wind and the waves obey him!"

Luke 8:24-25 The followers went to Jesus and woke him, saying, "Master! Master! We will drown!"

Jesus got up and gave a command to the wind and the waves. They stopped, and it became calm. Jesus said to his followers, "Where is your faith?"

The followers were afraid and amazed and said to each other, "Who is this that commands even the wind and the water, and they obey him?"

John 13:3 Jesus knew that the Father had given him power over everything and that he had come from God and was going back to God.

Colossians 1:15-20 No one can see God, but Jesus Christ is exactly like him. He ranks higher than everything that has been made. Through his power all things were made—things in heaven and on earth, things seen and unseen, all powers, authorities, lords, and rulers. All things were made through Christ and for Christ. He was there before anything was made, and all things continue because of him. He is the head of the body, which is the church. Everything comes from him. He is the first one who was raised from the dead. So in all things Jesus has first place. God was pleased for all of himself to live in Christ. And through Christ, God has brought all things back to himself again—things on earth and things in heaven. God made peace through the blood of Christ's death on the cross.

Hebrews 2:5-18 God did not choose angels to be the rulers of the new world that was coming, which is what we have been talking about. It is written in the Scriptures,

"Why are people important to you?
Why do you take care of human beings?
You made them a little lower than the angels
And crowned them with glory and honor.
You put all things under their control." (Psalm 8:4-6)

When God put everything under their control, there was nothing left that they did not rule. Still, we do not yet see them ruling over everything. But we see Jesus, who for a short time was made lower than the angels. And now he is wearing a crown of glory and honor because he suffered and died. And by God's grace, he died for everyone.

God is the One who made all things, and all things are for his glory. He wanted to have many children share his glory, so he made the One who leads people to salvation perfect through suffering.

Jesus, who makes people holy, and those who are made holy are from the same family. So he is not ashamed to call them his brothers and sisters. He says,

"Then, I will tell my fellow Israelites about you;
I will praise you in the public meeting." (Psalm 22:22)

He also says,

"I will trust in God." (Isaiah 8:17)

And he also says,

"I am here, and with me are the children God has given me." (Isaiah 8:18)

Since these children are people with physical bodies, Jesus himself became like them. He did this so that, by dying, he could destroy the one who has the power of death—the devil—and free those who were like slaves all their lives because of their fear of death. Clearly, it is not angels that Jesus helps, but the people who are from Abraham. For this reason Jesus had to be made like his brothers in every way so he could be their merciful and faithful high priest in service to God. Then Jesus could bring forgiveness for their sins. And now he can help those who are tempted, because he himself suffered and was tempted.

Hebrews 4:14-16 Since we have a great high priest, Jesus the Son of God, who has gone into heaven, let us hold on to the faith we have. For our high priest is able to understand our weaknesses. When he lived on earth, he was tempted in every way that we are, but he did not sin. Let us, then, feel very sure that we can come before God's throne where there is grace. There we can receive mercy and grace to help us when we need it.

Hebrews 5:4-10 To be high priest is an honor, but no one chooses himself for this work. He must be called by God as Aaron was. So also Christ did not choose himself to have the honor of being a high priest, but God chose him. God said to him,

"You are my Son.
Today I have become your Father." (Psalm 2:7)
And in another Scripture God says,
"You are a priest forever,
a priest like Melchizedek." (Psalm 110:4)

While Jesus lived on earth, he prayed to God and asked God for help. He prayed with loud cries and tears to the One who could save him from death, and his prayer was heard because he trusted God. Even though Jesus was the Son of God, he learned obedience by what he suffered. And because his obedience was perfect, he was able to give eternal salvation to all who obey him. In this way God made Jesus a high priest, a priest like Melchizedek.

Acts 17:30-31 "In the past, people did not understand God, and he ignored this. But now, God tells all people in the world to change their hearts and lives. God has set a day that he will judge all the world with fairness, by the man he chose long ago. And God has proved this to everyone by raising that man from the dead!"

1 Corinthians 15:25-28 Christ must rule until he puts all enemies under his control. The last enemy to be destroyed will be death. The Scripture says that God put all things under his control. When it says "all things" are under him, it is clear this does not include God himself. God is the One who put everything under his control. After everything has been put under the Son, then he will put himself under God, who had put all things under him. Then God will be the complete ruler over everything.

God And Jesus Are One

Colossians 1:15-20 No one can see God, but Jesus Christ is exactly like him. He ranks higher than everything that has been made. Through his power all things were made—things in heaven and on earth, things seen and unseen, all powers, authorities, lords, and rulers. All things were made through Christ and for Christ. He was there before anything was made, and all things continue because of him. He is the head of the body, which is the church. Everything comes from him. He is the first one who was raised from the dead. So in all things Jesus has first place. God was pleased for all of himself to live in Christ. And through Christ, God has brought all things back to himself again—things on earth and things in heaven. God made peace through the blood of Christ's death on the cross.

Colossians 2:9-10 All of God lives in Christ fully (even when Christ was on earth), and you have a full and true life in Christ, who is ruler over all rulers and powers.

Hebrews 1:1-14 In the past God spoke to our ancestors through the prophets many times and in many different ways. But now in these last days God has spoken to us through his Son. God has chosen his Son to own all things, and through him he made the world. The Son reflects the glory of God and shows exactly what God is like. He holds everything together with his powerful word. When the Son made people clean from their sins, he sat down at the right side of God, the Great One in heaven. The Son became much greater than the angels, and God gave him a name that is much greater than theirs.

2 Corinthians 4:4 The devil who rules this world has blinded the minds of those who do not believe. They cannot see the light of the Good News—the Good News about the glory of Christ, who is exactly like God.

John 8:23-30 Jesus said, "You people are from here below, but I am from above. You belong to this world, but I don't belong to this world. So I told you that you would die in your sins. Yes, you will die in your sins if you don't believe that I am he."

They asked, "Then who are you?"

Jesus answered, "I am what I have told you from the beginning. I have many things to say and decide about you. But I tell people only the things I have heard from the One who sent me, and he speaks the truth."

The people did not understand that he was talking to them about the Father. So Jesus said to them, "When you lift up the Son of Man, you will know that I am he. You will know that these things I do are not by my own authority but that I say only what the Father has taught me. The One who sent me is with me. I always do what is pleasing to him, so he has not left me alone." While Jesus was saying these things, many people believed in him.

John 8:54-59 Jesus answered, "If I give honor to myself, that honor is worth nothing. The One who gives me honor is my Father, and you say he is your God. You don't really know him, but I know him. If I said I did not know him, I would be a liar like you. But I do know him and I obey what he says. Your father Abraham was very happy that he would see my day. He saw that day and was glad."

The Jews said to him, "You have never seen Abraham! You are not even fifty years old."

Jesus answered, "I tell you the truth, before Abraham was even born, I am!" When Jesus said this, the people picked up stones to throw at him. But Jesus hid himself, and then he left the Temple.

2 Peter 1-3 From Simon Peter, a servant and apostle of Jesus Christ. To you who have received a faith as valuable as ours, because our God and Savior Jesus Christ does what is right. Grace and peace be given to you more and more, because you truly know God and Jesus our Lord.

Jesus has the power of God, by which he has given us everything we need to live and to serve God. We have these things because we know him. Jesus called us by his glory and goodness.

Acts 2:36 "So, all the people of Israel should know this truly: God has made Jesus—the man you nailed to the cross—both Lord and Christ."

Matthew 10:40 "Whoever accepts you also accepts me, and whoever accepts me also accepts the One who sent me."

Mark 6:49-50 But when they saw him walking on the water, they thought he was a ghost and cried out. They all saw him and were afraid. But quickly Jesus spoke to them and said, "**Have courage! It is I. Do not be afraid**."

Luke 4:18 "The Lord has put his Spirit in me,
    because he appointed me to tell the Good News to the poor.
He has sent me to tell the captives they are free
    and to tell the blind that they can see again. (Isaiah 61:1)
God sent me to free those who have been treated unfairly (Isaiah 58:6)
And to announce the time when the Lord will show his kindness."

John 1:18 No one has ever seen God. But God the only Son is very close to the Father, and he has shown us what God is like.

John 5:30-47 "I can do nothing alone. I judge only the way I am told, so my judgment is fair. I don't try to please myself, but I try to please the One who sent me.

"If only I tell people about myself, what I say is not true. But there is another who tells about me, and I know that the things he says about me are true.

"You have sent people to John, and he has told you the truth. It is not that I accept such human telling; I tell you this so you can be saved. John was like a burning and shining lamp, and you were happy to enjoy his light for a while.

"But I have a proof about myself that is greater than that of John. The things I do, which are the things my Father gave me to do, prove that the Father sent me. And the Father himself who sent me has given proof about me. You have never heard his voice or seen what he looks like. His teaching does not live in you, because you don't believe in the One the Father sent. You carefully study the Scriptures because you think they give you eternal life. They do in fact tell about me, but you refuse to come to me to have that life.

"I don't need praise from people. But I know you — I know that you don't have God's love in you. **I have come from my Father and speak for him, but you don't accept me**. But when another person comes, speaking only for himself, you will accept him. You try to get praise from each other, but you do not try to get the praise that comes from the only God. So how can you believe? Don't think that I will stand before the Father and say you are wrong. The one who says you are wrong is Moses, the one you hoped would save you. If you really believed Moses, you would believe me, because Moses wrote about me. But if you don't believe what Moses wrote, how can you believe what I say?"

John 6:43-51 (Jesus is the bread that gives life.) But Jesus answered, "Stop complaining to each other. The Father is the One who sent me. No one can come to me unless the Father draws him to me, and I will raise that person up on the last day. It is written in the prophets, 'They will all be taught by God.' Everyone who listens to the Father and learns from him comes to me. No one has seen the Father except the one who is from God; only he has seen the Father. I tell you the truth, whoever believes has eternal life. I am the bread that gives life. Your ancestors ate the manna in the desert, but still they died. Here is the bread that comes down from heaven. Anyone who eats this bread will never die. I am the living bread that came down from heaven. Anyone who eats this bread will live forever. This bread is my flesh, which I will give up so that the world may have life."

John 10:30 "The Father and I are one."

John 12:44-50 Then Jesus cried out, "Whoever believes in me is really believing in the One who sent me. **Whoever sees me sees the One who sent me**. I have come as light into the world so that whoever believes in me would not stay in darkness.

"Anyone who hears my words and does not obey them, I do not judge, because I did not come to judge the world, but to save the world. There is a judge for those who refuse to believe in me and do not accept my words. The word I have taught will be their judge on the last day. The things I taught were not from myself. The Father who sent me told me what to say and what to teach. And I know that eternal life comes from what the Father commands. So whatever I say is what the Father told me to say."

John 14:8-14 Philip said to him, "Lord, show us the Father. That is all we need."

Jesus answered, "I have been with you a long time now. Do you still not know me, Philip? Whoever has seen me has seen the Father. So why do you say, 'Show us the Father'? Don't you believe that I am in the Father and the Father is in me? The words I say to you don't come from me, but the Father lives in me and does his own work. **Believe me when I say that I am in the Father and the Father is in me**. Or believe because of the miracles I have done. I tell you the truth, whoever believes in me will do the same things that I do. Those who believe will do even greater things than these, because I am going to the Father. And if you ask for anything in my name, I will do it for you so that the Father's glory will be shown through the Son, If you ask me for anything in my name, I will do it."

John 14:20-21 "On that day you will know that I am in my Father, and that you are in me and I am in you. Those who know my commands and obey them are the ones who love me, and my Father will love those who love me. I will love them and will show myself to them."

John 16:1-15 "I have told you these things to keep you from giving up. People will put you out of their synagogues. Yes, the time is coming when those who kill you will think they are offering service to God. They will do this because they have not known the Father and they have not known me. I have told you these things now so that when the time comes you will remember that I warned you.

"I did not tell you these things at the beginning, because I was with you then. Now I am going back to the One who sent me. But none of you asks me, 'Where are you going?' You hearts are filled with sadness because I have told you these things. But I tell you the truth, it is better for you that I go away. When I go away, I will send the Helper to you. If I do not go away, the Helper will not come. When the Helper comes, he will prove to the people of the world the truth about sin, about being right with God, and about judgment. He will prove to them that sin is not believing in me. He will prove to them that being right with God comes from my going to the Father and not being seen anymore. And the Helper will prove to them that judgment happened when the ruler of this world was judged.

"I have many more things to say to you, but they are too much for you now. But when the Spirit of truth comes, he will lead you into all truth. He will not speak his own words, but he will speak only what he hears, and he will tell you what is to come. The Spirit of truth will bring glory to me, because he will take what I have to say and tell it to you. **All that the Father has is mine**. That is why I said that the Spirit will take what I have to say and tell it to you."

John 16:25-33 "I have told you these things, using stories that hide the meaning. But the time will come when I will not use stories like that to tell you things; I will speak to you in plain words about the Father. In that day you will ask the Father for things in my name. I mean, I will not need to ask the Father for you. The Father himself loves you. He loves you because you loved me and believed that I came from God. I came from the Father into the world. Now I am leaving the world and going back to the Father."

Then the followers of Jesus said, "You are speaking clearly to us now and are not using stories that are hard to understand. We can see now that you know all things. You can answer a person's question even before it is asked. This makes us believe you came from God."

Jesus answered, "So now you believe? Listen to me; a time is coming when you will be scattered, each to his own home. That time is now here. You will leave me alone, but I am never really alone, because the Father is with me.

"I told you these things so that you can have peace in me. In this world you will have trouble, but be Brave! I have defeated the world."

John 17:1-26 After Jesus said these things, he looked toward heaven and prayed, "Father, the time has come. Give glory to your Son so that the Son can give glory to you. You gave the Son power over all people so that the Son could give eternal life to all those you gave him. And this is eternal life; that people know you, the only true God, and that they know Jesus Christ, the One you sent. Having finished the work you gave me to do, I brought you glory on earth. And now, Father, give me glory with you; give me the glory I had with you before the world was made.

"I showed what you are like to those you gave me from the world. They belonged to you, and you gave them to me, and they have obeyed your teaching.

Now they know that everything you gave me comes from you. I gave them the teachings you gave me, and they accepted them. They know that I truly came from you, and they believed that you sent me. I am praying for them. I am not praying for people in the world but for those you gave me, because they are yours. All I have is yours, and all you have is mine. And my glory is shown through them. I am coming to you; I will not stay in the world any longer. But they are still in the world. Holy Father, keep them safe by the power of your name, the name you gave me, so that they will be one, just as you and I are one. While I was with them, I kept them safe by the power of your name, the name you gave me. I protected them, and only one of them, the one worthy of destruction, was lost so that the Scripture would come true.

"I am coming to you now. But I pray these things while I am still in the world so that these followers can have all of my joy in them. I have given them your teaching. And the world has hated them, because they don't belong to the world just as I don't belong to the world. I am not asking you to take them out of the world but to keep them safe from the Evil One. They don't belong to the world, just as I don't belong to the world. Make them ready for your service through your truth; your teaching is truth. I have sent them into the world, just as you sent me into the world. For their sake, I am making myself ready to serve so that they can be ready for their service of the truth.

"I pray for these followers, but I am also praying for all those who will believe in me because of their teaching. Father, I pray that they can be one. **As you are in me and I am in you,** I pray that they can also be one in us. Then the world will believe that you sent me. **I have given these people the glory that you gave me so that they can be one, just as you and I are one**. **I will be in them and you will be in me so that they will be completely one**. Then the world will know that you sent me and that you loved them just as much as you loved me.

"Father, I want these people that you gave me to be with me where I am. I want them to see my glory, which you gave me because you loved me before the world was made. Father, you are the One who is good. The world does not know you, but I know you, and these people know you sent me. I showed them what you are like, and I will show them again. Then they will have the same love that you have for me, and I will live in them."

Philippians 2:5-11 In your lives you must think and act like Christ Jesus. Christ himself was like God in everything.

> But he did not think that being equal with God was something to be
> used for his own benefit.

But he gave up his place with God and made himself nothing.

> He was born to be a man
> and become like a servant.

And when he was living as a man,
>he humbled himself and was fully obedient to God,
>even when that caused his death—death on a cross.

So God raised him to the highest place.
>God made his name greater than every other name

so that every knee will bow to the name of Jesus—
>everyone in heaven, on earth, and under the earth.

And everyone will confess that Jesus Christ is Lord
>and bring glory to God the Father.

Through Christ Only Can We Reach God

I Timothy 2:5-6 There is one God and one way human beings can reach God. That way is through Christ Jesus, who is himself human. He gave himself as a payment to free all people. He is proof that came at the right time.

John 14:6-7 Jesus answered, "I am the way, and the truth, and the life. The only way to the Father is through me. If you really knew me, you would know my Father, too. But now you do know him, and you have seen him."

Ephesians 1:9-10 Let us know his secret purpose. This was what God wanted, and he planned to do it through Christ. His goal was to carry out his plan, when the right time came, that all things in heaven and on earth would be joined together in Christ as the head.

All Good Comes From God: God Does Not Tempt Us

James 1:13-15 When people are tempted, they should not say, "God is tempting me." Evil cannot tempt God, and God himself does not tempt anyone. But people are tempted when their own evil desire leads them away and traps them. This desire leads to sin, and then the sin grows and brings death.

James 1:16-18 My dear brothers and sisters, do not be fooled about this. Every good action and every perfect gift is from God. These good gifts come down from the Creator of the sun, moon, and stars, who does not change like their shifting shadows. God decided to give us life through the word of truth so we might be the most important of all the things he made.

Romans 8:28 We know that in everything God works for the good of those who love him. They are the people he called, because that was his plan.

I Corinthians 10:13 The only temptation that has come to you is that which everyone has. But you can trust God, who will not permit you to be tempted more than you can stand. But when you are tempted, he will also give you a way to escape so that you will be able to stand it.

All Scripture Is From God

2 Timothy 3:16-17 All Scripture is given by God and is useful for teaching, for showing people what is wrong in their lives, for correcting faults, and for teaching how to live right. Using the Scriptures, the person who serves God will be capable, having all that is needed to do every good work.

2 Peter 1:20-21 Most of all, you must understand this: No prophecy in the Scriptures ever comes from the prophet's own interpretation. No prophecy ever came from what a person wanted to say, but people led by the Holy Spirit spoke words from God.

Exodus 4:11-12 Then the Lord said to him, "Who made a person's mouth? And who makes someone deaf or not able to speak? Or who gives a person sight or blindness? **It is I, the Lord**. Now go! I will help you speak, and I will teach you what to say."

Exodus 34:27 Then the Lord said to Moses, "Write down these words, because with these words I have made an agreement with you and Israel."

Jeremiah 1:9 Then the Lord reached out his hand and touched my mouth. He said to me, "See, I am putting my words in your mouth."

Micah 1:1 During the time that Jotham, Ahaz, and Hezekiah were kings of Judah, the word of the Lord came to Micah, who was from Moresheth. He saw these visions about Samaria and Jerusalem.

Homosexuality

Romans 1:26-27 Because people did those things, God left them and let them do the shameful things they wanted to do. Women stopped having natural sex and started having sex with other women. In the same way, men stopped having natural sex and began wanting each other. Men did shameful things with other men, and in their bodies they received the punishment for those wrongs.

I Corinthians 6:9-10 Surely you know that the people who do wrong will not inherit God's kingdom. Do not be fooled. Those who sin sexually, worship idols, take part in adultery, those who are male prostitutes, or men who have sexual relations with other men, those who steal, are greedy, get drunk, lie about others, or rob—these people will not inherit God's kingdom.

I Timothy 1:9-10 We also know that the law is not made for good people but for those who are against the law and for those who refuse to follow it. It is for people who are against God and are sinful, who are not holy and have no religion, who kill their fathers and mothers, who murder, who take part in sexual sins, who have sexual relations with people of the same sex, who sell slaves, who tell lies, who speak falsely, and who do anything against the true teaching of God.

Conscience

Hebrews 9:14 How much more is done by the blood of Christ. He offered himself through the eternal Spirit as a perfect sacrifice to God. His blood will make our consciences pure from useless acts so we may serve the living God.

Hebrews 9:9 This is an example for the present time. It shows that the gifts and sacrifices offered cannot make the conscience of the worshiper perfect.

Hebrews 10:22 Let us come near to God with a sincere heart and a sure faith, because we have been made free from a guilty conscience, and our bodies have been washed with pure water.

Hebrews 13:18 Pray for us. We are sure that we have a clear conscience, because we always want to do the right thing.

I John 3:19-24 This is the way we know that we belong to the way of truth. When our hearts make us feel guilty, we can still have peace before God. God is greater than our hearts, and he knows everything. My dear friends, if our hearts do not make us feel guilty, we can come without fear into God's presence. And God gives us what we ask for because we obey God's commands and do what pleases him. This is what God commands: that we believe in his Son, Jesus Christ, and that we love each other, just as he commanded. The people who obey God's commands live in God, and God lives in them. We know that God lives in us because of the Spirit God gave us.

Romans 9:1 I am in Christ, and I am telling you the truth; I do not lie. My conscience is ruled by the Holy Spirit, and it tells me I am not lying.

Titus 1:15 To those who are pure, all things are pure, but to those who are full of sin and do not believe, nothing is pure. Both their minds and their consciences have been ruined.

1 Peter 3:15-16 But respect Christ as the holy Lord in your hearts. Always be ready to answer everyone who asks you to explain about the hope you have, but answer in a gentle way and with respect. Keep a clear conscience so that those who speak evil of your good life in Christ will be made ashamed.

1 Peter 3:21 And that water is like baptism that now saves you—not the washing of dirt from the body, but the promise made to God from a good conscience. And this is because Jesus Christ was raised from the dead.

1 Timothy 1:5 The purpose of this command is for people to have love, a love that comes from a pure heart and a good conscience and a true faith.

1 Timothy 3:9 With a clear conscience they must follow the secret of the faith that God made known to us.

1 Timothy 4:1-2 Now the Holy Spirit clearly says that in the later times some people will stop believing the faith. They will follow spirits that lie and teachings of demons. Such teachings come from the false words of liars whose consciences are destroyed as if by hot iron.

Going To Church

Hebrews 10:25 You should not stay away from the church meetings, as some are doing, but you should meet together and encourage each other. Do this even more as you see the day coming.

Acts 10:35 "In every country God accepts anyone who worships him and does what is right."

Breaking One Command Is Breaking All The Commands

James 2:10 A person who follows all of God's law but fails to obey even one command is guilty of breaking all the commands in that law.

Loving God Is Obeying His Commands

I John 5:1-5 Everyone who believes that Jesus is the Christ is God's child, and whoever loves the Father also loves the Father's children. This is how we know we love God's children: when we love God and obey his commands. **Loving God means obeying his commands.** And God's commands are not too hard for us, because everyone who is a child of God conquers the world. And this is the victory that conquers the world—our faith. So the one who wins against the world is the person who believes that Jesus is the Son of God.

Luke 6:46-49 "Why do you call me, 'Lord, Lord,' but do not do what I say? I will show you what everyone is like who comes to me and hears my words and obeys. That person is like a man building a house who dug deep and laid the foundation on rock. When the floods came, the water tried to wash the house away, but it could not shake it, because the house was built well. But the one who hears my words and does not obey is like a man who built his house on the ground without a foundation. When the floods came, the house quickly fell and was completely destroyed."

Matthew 7:24-27 Same as above with variations.

We Should Not Pray Or Do Good Things
In Front Of People For Praise

Matthew 6:1-6 "Be careful! When you do good things, don't do them in front of people to be seen by them. If you do that, you will have no reward from your Father in heaven.

"When you give to the poor, don't be like the hypocrites. They blow trumpets in the synagogues and on the streets so that people will see them and honor them. I tell you the truth, those hypocrites already have their full reward. So when you give to the poor, don't let anyone know what you are doing. Your giving should be done in secret. Your Father can see what is done in secret, and he will reward you.

"When you pray, don't be like the hypocrites. They love to stand in the synagogues and on the street corners and pray so people will see them. I tell you the truth, they already have their full reward. When you pray, you should go into your room and close the door and pray to your Father who cannot be seen. Your Father can see what is done in secret, and he will reward you."

John The Baptist Is Elijah

Matthew 11:7-15 As John's followers were leaving, Jesus began talking to the people about John. Jesus said, "What did you go out into the desert to see? A reed blown by the wind? What did you go out to see? A man dressed in fine clothes? No, those who wear fine clothes live in kings' palaces. So why did you go out? To see a prophet? Yes, and I tell you, John is more than a prophet. This was written about him:

> 'I will send my messenger ahead of you,
> who will prepare the way for you.' (Malachi 3:1)

I tell you the truth, John the Baptist is greater than any other person ever born, but even the least important person in the kingdom of heaven is greater than John. Since the time John the Baptist came until now, the kingdom of heaven has been going forward in strength, and people have been trying to take it by force. All the prophets and the law of Moses told about what would happen until the time John came. And if you will believe what they said, you will believe that John is Elijah, whom they said would come. You people who can hear me, listen!"

Mark 9:12-13 Jesus answered, "They are right to say that Elijah must come first and make everything the way it should be. But why does the Scripture say that the Son of Man will suffer much and that people will treat him as if he were nothing? I tell you that Elijah has already come. And people did to him whatever they wanted to do, just as the Scriptures said it would happen."

Luke 7:24-28 When John's followers left, Jesus began talking to the people about John: "What did you go out into the desert to see? A reed blown by the wind? What did you go out to see? A man dressed in fine clothes? No, people who have fine clothes and much wealth live in kings' palaces. But what did you go out to see? A prophet? Yes, and I tell you, John is more than a prophet. This was written about him:

> 'I will send my messenger ahead of you,
> who will prepare the way for you.' (Malachi 3:1)

I tell you, John is greater than any other person ever born, but even the least important person in the kingdom of God is greater than John."

Old Agreement And Circumcision

Genesis 9: 8-13 Then God said to Noah and his sons, "Now I am making my agreement with you and your people who will live after you, and with every living thing that is with you—the bird, the tame and the wild animals, and with everything that came out of the boat with you—with every living thing on earth. I make this agreement with you: I will never again destroy all living things by a flood. A flood will never again destroy the earth."

And God said, "This is the sign of the agreement between me and you and every living creature that is with you. I am putting my rainbow in the clouds as the sign of the agreement between me and the earth."

Genesis 15:4-6 Then the Lord spoke his word to Abram: "He will not be the one to inherit what you have. You will have a son of your own who will inherit what you have."

Then God led Abram outside and said, "Look at the sky. There are so many stars you cannot count them. Your descendants also will be too many to count."

Abram believed the Lord. And the Lord accepted Abram's faith, and that faith made him right with God.

Genesis 15:17-20 After the sun went down, it was very dark. Suddenly a smoking firepot and a blazing torch passed between the halves of the dead animals. So on that day the Lord made an agreement with Abram and said, "I will give to your descendants the land between the river of Egypt and the great river Euphrates. This is the land of the Kenites, Kenizzites, Kadmonites, Hittites, Perizzites, Rephaites, Amorites, Canaanites, Girgashites, and Jebusites."

Genesis 17:9-14 Then God said to Abraham, "You and your descendants must keep this agreement from now on. This is my agreement with you and all your descendants, which you must obey: Every male among you must be circumcised. Cut away your foreskin to show that you are prepared to follow the agreement between me and you. From now on when a baby boy is eight days old, you will circumcise him. This includes any boy born among your people or any who is your slave, who is not one of your descendants. Circumcise every baby boy whether he is born in your family or bought as a slave. Your bodies will be marked to show that you are part of my agreement that lasts forever. Any male who is not circumcised will be cut off from his people, because he has broken my agreement."

Genesis 22:1-18 After these things God tested Abraham's faith. God said to him, "Abraham!"

And he answered, "Here I am."

Then God said, "Take your only son, Isaac, the son you love, and go to the land of Moriah. Kill him there and offer him as a whole burnt offering on one of the mountains I will tell you about."

...Then Abraham took his knife and was about to kill his son.

But the angel of the Lord called to him from heaven and said, "Abraham! Abraham!"

Abraham answered, "Yes."

The angel said, "Don't kill your son or hurt him in any way. Now I can see that you trusted God and that you have not kept your son, your only son, from me."

Then Abraham looked up and saw a male sheep caught in a bush by its horns. So Abraham went and took the sheep and killed it. He offered it as a whole burnt offering to God, and his son was saved. So Abraham named that place The Lord Provides. Even today people say, "On the mountain of the Lord it will be provided."

The angel of the Lord called to Abraham from heaven a second time and said, "The Lord says, 'Because you did not keep back your son, your only son, from me, I make you this promise by my own name: I will surely bless you and give you many descendants. They will be as many as the stars in the sky and the sand on the seashore, and they will capture the cities of their enemies. **Through your descendants all the nations on the earth will be blessed, because you obeyed me.'**"

Leviticus 12:3 "'On the eighth day the boy must be circumcised.'"

New Agreement And Circumcision

2 Corinthians 3:4-6 We can say this, because through Christ we feel certain before God. We are not saying that we can do this work ourselves. It is God who makes us able to do all that we do. He made us able to be servants of a new agreement from himself to his people. This new agreement is not written law, but it is of the Spirit. The written law brings death, but the Spirit gives life.

Galatians 5:11 My brothers and sisters, I do not teach that a man must be circumcised. If I teach circumcision, why am I still being attacked? If I still taught circumcision, my preaching about the cross would not be a problem.

John 1:17 The law was given through Moses. But grace and truth came through Jesus Christ.

Philippians 3:2-3 Watch out for those who do evil, who are like dogs, who demand to cut the body. We are the ones who are truly circumcised. We worship God through his Spirit, and our pride is in Christ Jesus. We do not put trust in ourselves or anything we can do.

Colossians 2:11 Also in Christ you had a different kind of circumcision, a circumcision not done by hands. It was through Christ's circumcision, that is, his death, that you were made free from the power of your sinful self.

Colossians 3:11 In the new life there is no difference between Greeks and Jews, those who are circumcised and those who are not circumcised, or people who are foreigners, or Scythians. There is no difference between slaves and free people. But Christ is in all believers, and Christ is all that is important.

Hebrews 8: 6-12 But the priestly work that has been given to Jesus is much greater than the work that was given to the other priests. In the same way, the new agreement that Jesus brought from God to his people is much greater than the old one. And the new agreement is based on promises of better things.

If there had been nothing wrong with the first agreement, there would have been no need for a second agreement. But God found something wrong with his people. He says:

> "Look, the time is coming, says the Lord,
>   when I will make a new agreement
> with the people of Israel
>   and the people of Judah.

It will not be like the agreement
    I made with their ancestors
when I took them by the hand
    to bring them out of Egypt.
But they broke that agreement,
    and I turned away from them, says the Lord.
This is the agreement I will make
    with the people of Israel at that time, says the Lord.
I will put my teachings in their minds
    and write them on their hearts.
I will be their God,
    and they will be my people.
People will no longer have to teach their neighbors and relatives
    to know the Lord,
because all people will know me,
    from the least to the most important.
I will forgive them for the wicked things they did,
    and I will not remember their sins anymore. (Jeremiah 31:31-34)

Matthew 26:27-29 Then Jesus took a cup and thanked God for it and gave it to the followers. He said, "Every one of you drink this. This is my blood which is the new agreement that God makes with his people. This blood is poured out for many to forgive their sins. I tell you this: I will not drink of this fruit of the vine again until that day when I drink it new with you in my Father's kingdom."
    Mark 14:24 Same as above with variations.
    Luke 22:20 Same as above with variations.
    I Corinthians 11:25 Same as above with variations.

Luke 12:54-56 (The Jews missed the signs of Jesus) Then Jesus said to the people, "When you see clouds coming up in the west, you say, 'It's going to rain,' and it happens. When you feel the wind begin to blow from the south, you say, 'It will be a hot day,' and it happens. Hypocrites! You know how to understand the appearance of the earth and sky. Why don't you understand what is happening now?"

Romans 4:9-12 Is this blessing only for those who are circumcised or also for those who are not circumcised? We have already said that God accepted Abraham's faith and that faith made him right with God. So how did this happen? Did God accept Abraham before or after he was circumcised? It was before his circumcision. Abraham was circumcised to show that he was right with God through faith before he was circumcised. So Abraham is the father of all those who believe but are not circumcised; he is the father of all believers who are accepted as being right with God. And Abraham is also the father of those who have been circumcised and who live following the faith that our father Abraham had before he was circumcised.

The Old Agreement Versus The New Agreement

Hebrews 9:1-10 The first agreement had rules for worship and a man-made place for worship. The Holy Tent was set up for this....

When everything in the Tent was made ready in this way, the priests went into the first room every day to worship. But only the high priest could go into the second room, and he did that only once a year. He could never enter the inner room without taking blood with him, which he offered to God for himself and for sins the people did without knowing they did them. The Holy Spirit uses this to show that the way into the Most Holy Place was not open while the system of the old Holy Tent was still being used. This is an example for the present time. It shows that the gifts and sacrifices offered cannot make the conscience of the worshiper perfect. These gifts and sacrifices were only about food and drink and special washings. They were rules for the body, to be followed until the time of God's new way.

Hebrews 9:11-22 But when Christ came as the high priest of the good things we now have, he entered the greater and more perfect tent. It is not made by humans and does not belong to this world. Christ entered the Most Holy Place only once—and for all time. He did not take with him the blood of goats and calves. His sacrifice was his own blood, and by it he set us free from sin forever. The blood of goats and bulls and the ashes of a cow are sprinkled on the people who are unclean, and this makes their bodies clean again. How much more is done by the blood of Christ. He offered himself through the eternal Spirit as a perfect sacrifice to God. His blood will make our consciences pure from useless acts so we may serve the living God.

For this reason Christ brings a new agreement from God to his people. Those who are called by God can now receive the blessings he has promised, blessings that will last forever. They can have those things because Christ died so that the people who lived under the first agreement could be set free from sin.

When there is a will it must be proven that the one who wrote that will is dead. A will means nothing while the person is alive; it can be used only after the person dies. This is why even the first agreement could not begin without blood to show death. First, Moses told all the people every command in the law. Next he took the blood of calves and mixed it with water. Then he used red wool and a branch of the hyssop plant to sprinkle it on the book of the law and on all the people. He said, "This is the blood that begins the Agreement that God commanded you to obey." In the same way, Moses sprinkled the blood on the Holy Tent and over all the things used in worship. The law says that almost everything must be made clean by blood, and sins cannot be forgiven without blood to show death.

Matthew 9:14-17 Then the followers of John came to Jesus and said, "Why do we and the Pharisees often give up eating for a certain time, but your followers don't?"

Jesus answered, "The friends of the bridegroom are not sad while he is with them. But the time will come when the bridegroom will be taken from them, and then they will give up eating.

"No one sews a patch of unshrunk cloth over a hole in an old coat. If he does, the patch will shrink and pull away from the coat, making the hole worse. Also, people never pour new wine into old leather bags. Otherwise, the bags will break, the wine will spill, and the wine bags will be ruined. But people always pour new wine into new wine bags. Then both will continue to be good."

Mark 2:21-22 Same as above with variations.

Luke 5:33-39 Same as above with variations.

Matthew 23:23-26 "How terrible for you, teachers of the law and Pharisees! You are hypocrites! You give to God one-tenth of everything you earn—even your mint, dill, and cumin. But you don't obey the really important teaching of the law—justice, mercy, and being loyal. These are the things you should do, as well as those other things. You guide the people but your are blind. You are like a person who picks a fly out of a drink and then swallows a camel.

"How terrible for you, teachers of the law and Pharisees! You are hypocrites! You wash the outside of your cups and dishes, but inside they are full of things you got by cheating others and by pleasing only yourselves. Pharisees, you are blind! First make the inside of the cup clean, and then the outside of the cup can be truly clean."

Matthew 27:50-51 But Jesus cried out again in a loud voice and died. Then the curtain in the Temple was torn into two pieces, from the top to the bottom. Also, the earth shook and rocks broke apart.

Mark 15:37-39 Same as above with variations.

Mark 7:17-23 When Jesus left the people and went into the house, his followers asked him about this story. Jesus said, "Do you still not understand? Surely you know that nothing that enters someone from the outside can make that person unclean. It does not go into the mind, but into the stomach. Then it goes out of the body." (When Jesus said this, he meant that no longer was any food unclean for people to eat.)

And Jesus said, "The things that come out of people are the things that make them unclean. All these evil things begin inside people, in the mind: evil thoughts, sexual sins, stealing, murder, adultery, greed, evil actions, lying, doing sinful things, jealousy, speaking evil of others, pride, and foolish living. All these evil things come from inside and make people unclean."

Luke 11:37-54 Same as above with variations.

Romans 3:19-20 We know that the law's commands are for those who have the law. This stops all excuses and brings the whole world under God's judgment, because no one can be made right with God by following the law. The law only shows us our sin.

Romans 4:13-15 Abraham and his descendants received the promise that they would get the whole world. He did not receive that promise through the law, but through being right with God by his faith. If people could receive what God promised by following the law, then faith is worthless. And God's promise to Abraham is worthless, because the law can only bring God's anger. But if there is no law, there is nothing to disobey.

Romans 9:30-33 So what does all this mean? Those who are not Jews were not trying to make themselves right with God, but they were made right with God because of their faith. The people of Israel tried to follow a law to make themselves right with God. But they did not succeed, because they tried to make themselves right by the things they did instead of trusting in God to make them right. They stumbled over the stone that causes people to stumble. As it is written in Scripture:

> "I will put in Jerusalem a stone that causes people
>   to stumble,
> a rock that makes them fall.
> Anyone who trusts in him will never be
>   disappointed." (Isaiah 8:14; 28:16)

Romans 10:1-4 Brothers and sisters, the thing I want most is for all the Jews to be saved. That is my prayer to God. I can say this about them: They really try to follow God, but they do not know the right way. Because they did not know the way that God makes people right with him, they tried to make themselves right in their own way. So they did not accept God's way of making people right. Christ ended the law so that everyone who believes in him may be right with God.

Galatians 2:15-21 We were not born as non-Jewish "sinners," but as Jews. Yet we know that a person is made right with God not by following the law, but by trusting in Jesus Christ. So we, too, have put our faith in Christ Jesus, that we might be made right with God because we trusted in Christ. It is not because we followed the law, because no one can be made right with God by following the law.

We Jews came to Christ, trying to be made right with God, and it became clear that we are sinners, too. Does this mean that Christ encourages sin? No! But I would really be wrong to begin teaching again those things that I gave up. It was the law that put me to death, and I died to the law so that I can now live for God. I was put to death on the cross with Christ, and I do not live anymore—it is Christ who lives in me. I still live in my body, but I live by faith in the Son of God who loved me and gave himself to save me. By saying these things I am not going against God's grace. Just the opposite, if the law could make us right with God, then Christ's death would be useless.

Galatians 3:1-29 You people in Galatia were told very clearly about the death of Jesus Christ on the cross. But you were foolish; you let someone trick you. Tell me this one thing: How did you receive the Holy Spirit? Did you receive the Spirit by following the law? No, you received the Spirit because you heard the Good News and believed it. You began your life in Christ by the Spirit. Now are you trying to make it complete by your own power? That is foolish. Were all your experiences wasted? I hope not! Does God give you the Spirit and work miracles among you because you follow the law? No, he does these things because you heard the Good News and believed it.

The Scriptures say the same thing about Abraham. "Abraham believed God, and God accepted Abraham's faith, and that faith make him right with God." **So you should know that the true children of Abraham are those who have faith. The Scriptures, telling what would happen in the future, said that God would make the non-Jewish people right through their faith. This Good News was told to Abraham beforehand, as the Scripture says: "All nations will be blessed through you." So all who believe as Abraham believed are blessed just as Abraham was.** But those who depend on following the law to make them right are under a curse, because the Scriptures say, "Anyone will be cursed who does not always obey what is written in the Book of the Law." Now it is clear that no one can be made right with God by the law, because the Scriptures say, "Those who are right with God will live by trusting in him." **The law is not based on faith**. It says, "A person who obeys these things will live because of them." **Christ took away the curse the law put on us. He changed places with us and put himself under that curse**. It is written in the Scriptures, "Anyone whose body is displayed on a tree is cursed." Christ did this so that God's blessing promised to Abraham might come through Jesus Christ to those who are not Jews. Jesus died so that by our believing we could receive the Spirit that God promised.

Brothers and sisters, let us think in human terms: Even an agreement made between two persons is firm. After that agreement is accepted by both people, no one can stop it or add anything to it. **God made promises both to Abraham and to his descendant. God did not say, "and to your descendants." That** would mean many people. But God said, "and to your descendant." That means only one person; that person is Christ. This is what I mean: God had an agreement with Abraham and promised to keep it. The law, which came four hundred thirty years later, cannot change that agreement and so destroy God's promise to Abraham. If the law could give us Abraham's blessing, then the promise would not be necessary. But that is not possible, because God freely gave his blessings to Abraham through the promise he had made.

So what was the law for? It was given to show that the wrong things people do are against God's will. And it continued until the special descendant, who had been promised, came. The law was given through angels who used Moses for a mediator to give the law to people. But a mediator is not needed when there is only one side, and God is only one.

Does this mean that the law is against God's promises? Never! That would be true only if the law could make us right. But God did not give a law that can bring life. Instead, the Scriptures showed that the whole world is bound by sin. This was so the promise would be given through faith to people who believe in Jesus Christ.

Before this faith came, we were all held prisoners by the law. We had no freedom until God showed us the way of faith that was coming. In other words, the law was our guardian leading us to Christ so that we could be made right with God through faith. Now the way of faith has come, and we no longer live under a guardian.

You were all baptized into Christ, and so you were all clothed with Christ. This means that you are all children of God through faith in Christ Jesus. In Christ, there is no difference between Jew and Geek, slave and free person, male and female. You are all the same in Christ Jesus. You belong to Christ, so you are Abraham's descendants. You will inherit all of God's blessing because of the promise God made to Abraham.

Footnote: **Genesis 22: 18** *Through your descendant (seed = Christ) all nations on the earth will be blessed, because you obeyed me. Isaac = Christ. Abraham = God the Father who offered his son. Through faith we believe Christ saves us from our sins. Because of our faith in Christ we obey like Abraham did. Faith and believing without works is worth nothing. Even Abraham had to show his faith through works (the offering of his one and only son).*

Galatians 4:1-7 I want to tell you this: While those who will inherit their father's property are still children, they are no different from slaves. It does not matter that the children own everything. While they are children, they must obey those who are chosen to care for them. But when the children reach the age set by their fathers, they are free. It is the same for us. We were once like children, slaves to the useless rules of the world. But when the right time came, God sent his Son who was born of a woman and lived under the law. God did this so he could buy freedom for those who were under the law and so we could become his children.

Since you are God's children, God sent the Sprit of his Son into your hearts, and the Spirit cries out, "Father." So now you are not a slave; you are God's child, and God will give you the blessing he promised, because you are his child.

Galatians 4:21-31 Some of you still want to be under the law. Tell me, do you know what the law says? The Scriptures say that Abraham had two sons. The mother of one son was a slave woman, and the mother of the other son was a free woman. Abraham's son from the slave woman was born in the normal human way. But the son from the free woman was born because of the promise God made to Abraham.

This story teaches something else: The two women are like the two agreements between God and his people. One agreement is the law that God made on Mount Sinai, and the people who are under this agreement are like slaves. The mother named Hagar is like that agreement. She is like Mount Sinai in Arabia and is a picture of the earthy Jewish city of Jerusalem. This city and its people, the Jews, are slaves to the law. But the heavenly Jerusalem, which is above, is like the free woman, She is our mother. It is written in the Scriptures:

> "Be happy, Jerusalem.
> You are like a woman who never gave birth to children.
> Start singing and shout for joy.
> You never felt the pain of giving birth,
> but you will have more children
> than the woman who has a husband." (Isaiah 54:1)

My brothers and sisters, you are God's children because of his promise, as Isaac was then. The son who was born in the normal way treated the other son badly. It is the same today. But what does the Scripture say? "Throw out the slave woman and her son. The son of the slave woman should not inherit anything. The son of the free woman should receive it all." So my brothers and sister, we are not children of the slave woman, but of the free woman.

Galatians 5:1-15 We have freedom now, because Christ made us free. So stand strong. Do not change and go back into the slavery of the law. Listen, I Paul tell you that if you go back to the law by being circumcised, Christ does you no good. **Again, I warn every man: If you allow yourselves to be circumcised, you must follow all the law. If you try to be made right with God through the law, your life with Christ is over—you have left God's**

grace. But we have true hope that comes from being made right with God, and by the Spirit we wait eagerly for this hope. **When we are in Christ Jesus, it is not important if we are circumcised or not. The important thing is faith— the kind of faith that works through love**.

You were running a good race. Who stopped you from following the true way? This change did not come from the One who chose you. Be careful! Just a little yeast makes the whole batch of dough rise. But I trust in the Lord that you will not believe those different ideas. Whoever is confusing you with such ideas will be punished.

My brothers and sisters, I do not teach that a man must be circumcised. If I teach circumcision, why am I still being attacked? If I still taught circumcision, my preaching about the cross would not be a problem. I wish the people who are bothering you would castrate themselves!

My brothers and sisters, God called you to be free, but do not use your freedom as an excuse to do what pleases your sinful self. Serve each other with love. The whole law is made complete in this one command: Love your neighbor as you love yourself. If you go on hurting each other and tearing each other apart, be careful, or you will completely destroy each other.

Ephesians 2:11-18 You were not born Jewish. You are the people the Jews call "uncircumcised." Those who call you "uncircumcised" call themselves "circumcised." (Their circumcision is only something they themselves do on their bodies.) Remember that in the past you were without Christ. You were not citizens of Israel, and you had no part in the agreements with the promise that God made to his people. You had no hope, and you did not know God. But now in Christ Jesus, you who were far away from God are brought near through the blood of Christ's death. Christ himself is our peace. He made both Jewish people and those who are not Jews one people. They were separated as if there were a wall between them, but Christ broke down that wall of hate by giving his own body. The Jewish law had many commands and rules, but Christ ended that law. His purpose was to make the two groups of people become one new people in him and in this way make peace. It was also Christ's purpose to end the hatred between the two groups, to make them into one body, and to bring them back to God. Christ did all this with his death on the cross. Christ came and preached peace to you who were far away from God, and to those who were near to God. Yes, it is through Christ we all have the right to come to the Father in one Spirit.

Hebrews 7:11-28 The people were given the law based on a system of priests from the tribe of Levi, but they could not be made perfect through that system. So there was a need for another priest to come, a priest like Melchizedek, not Aaron. And when a different king of priest comes, the law must be changed, too. We are saying these things about Christ, who belonged to a different tribe. No one from that tribe ever served as a priest at the altar. It is clear that our Lord came from the tribe of Judah, and Moses said nothing about priests belonging to that tribe.

And this becomes even more clear when we see that another priest comes who is like Melchizedek. He was not made a priest by human rules and laws but through the power of his life, which continues forever. It is said about him,

> "You are a priest forever,
> a priest like Melchizedek." (Psalm 110:4)

The old rule is now set aside, because it was weak and useless. The law of Moses could not make anything perfect. But now a better hope has been given to us, and with this hope we can come near to God. It is important that God did this with an oath. Others became priests without an oath, but Christ became a priest with God's oath. God said:

> "The Lord has made a promise
> and will not change his mind.
> 'You are a priest forever.'" (Psalm 110:4)

This means that Jesus is the guarantee of a better agreement from God to his people.

When one of the other priests died, he could not continue being a priest. So there were many priests. But because Jesus lives forever, he will never stop serving as priest. So he is able always to save those who come to God through him because he always lives, asking God to help them.

Jesus is the kind of high priest we need. He is holy, sinless, pure, not influenced by sinners, and he is raised above the heavens. He is not like the other priests who had to offer sacrifices every day, first for their own sins, and then for the sins of the people. Christ offered his sacrifice only once and for all time when he offered himself. The law chooses high priests who are people with weaknesses, but the word of God's oath came later than the law. It made God's Son to be the high priest, and that Son has been made perfect forever.

Hebrews 8:6-13 But the priestly work that has been given to Jesus is much greater than the work that was given to the other priests. In the same way, the new agreement that Jesus brought from God to his people is much greater than the old one. And the new agreement is based on promises of better things. If there had been nothing wrong with the first agreement, there would have been no need for a second agreement. But God found something wrong with his people. He says:

> "Look, the time is coming, says the Lord,
>   when I will make a new agreement
>   with the people of Israel
>   and the people of Judah.
> It will not be like the agreement
>   I made with their ancestors
>   when I took them by the hand
>   to bring them out of Egypt.
>   But they broke that agreement,
>   and I turned away from them, says the Lord.
> This is the agreement I will make
>   with the people of Israel at that time, says the Lord.
> I will put my teachings in their minds
>   and write them on their hearts.
> I will be their God,
>   and they will be my people.
> People will no longer have to teach their neighbors and relatives
>   to know the Lord,
> because all people will know me,
>   from the least to the most important.
> I will forgive them for the wicked things they did,
>   and I will not remember their sins anymore." (Jeremiah 31:31-34)

God called this a new agreement, so he has made the first agreement old. And anything that is old and worn out is ready to disappear.

Hebrews 10:1-4 The law is only an unclear picture of the good things coming in the future; it is not the real thing. The people under the law offer the same sacrifices every year, but these sacrifices can never make perfect those who come near to worship God. If the law could make them perfect, the sacrifices would have already stopped. The worshipers would be made clean, and they would no longer have a sense of sin. But these sacrifices remind them of their sins every year, because it is impossible for the blood of bulls and goats to take away sins.

Hebrews 10:19-23 So, brothers and sisters, we are completely free to enter the Most Holy Place without fear because of the blood of Jesus' death. We can enter through a new and living way that Jesus opened for us. It leads through the curtain—Christ's body. And since we have a great priest over God's house, let us come near to God with a sincere heart and a sure faith, because we have been made free from a guilty conscience, and our bodies have been washed with pure water. Let us hold firmly to the hope that we have confessed, because we can trust God to do what he promised.

Satan/Devil

Matthew 4:1-11 (The devil tempts Jesus and quotes Scripture)
Luke 4:1-13 Same as above with variations.

Luke 10:18 Jesus said, "I saw Satan fall like lightning from heaven."

2 Corinthians 4:4 The devil who rules this world has blinded the minds of those who do not believe. They cannot see the light of the Good News—the Good News about the glory of Christ, who is exactly like God.

2 Corinthians 11:14-15 This does not surprise us. Even Satan changes himself to look like an angel of light. So it does not surprise us if Satan's servants also make themselves look like servants who work for what is right. But in the end they will be punished for what they do.

Ephesians 6:10-18 Finally, be strong in the Lord and in his great power. Put on the full armor of God so that you can fight against the devil's evil tricks. Our fight is not against people on earth but against the rulers and authorities and the powers of this world's darkness, against the spiritual powers of evil in the heavenly world. That is why you need to put on God's full armor. Then on the day of evil you will be able to stand strong. And when you have finished the whole fight, you will still be standing. So stand strong, with the belt of truth tied around your waist and the protection of right living on your chest. On your feet wear the Good News of peace to help you stand strong. And also use the shield of faith with which you can stop all the burning arrows of the Evil One. Accepts God's salvation as your helmet, and take the sword of the Spirit, which is the word of God. Pray in the Spirit at all times with all kinds of prayers, asking for everything you need. To do this you must always be ready and never give up. Always pray for all God's people.

James 4:7 So give yourselves completely to God. Stand against the devil, and the devil will run from you.

I Peter 5:8-9 Control yourselves and be careful! The devil, your enemy, goes around like a roaring lion looking for someone to eat. Refuse to give in to him, by standing strong in your faith. You know that your Christian family all over the world is having the same kinds of suffering.

John 8:44-45 "You belong to your father the devil, and you want to do what he wants. He was a murderer from the beginning and was against the truth, because there is no truth in him. When he tells a lie, he shows what he is really like, because he is a liar and the father of lies. But because I speak the truth, you don't believe me."

Jesus Teaches The Good News And Heals People

Matthew 4:23-25 Jesus went everywhere in Galilee, teaching in the synagogues, preaching the Good News about the kingdom of heaven, and healing all the people's diseases and sicknesses. The news about Jesus spread all over Syria, and people brought all the sick to him. They were suffering from different kinds of diseases. Some were in great pain, some had demons, some were epileptics, and some were paralyzed. Jesus healed all of them. Many people from Galilee, the Ten Towns, Jerusalem, Judea, and the land across the Jordan River followed him.

Luke 4:16-21 Jesus traveled to Nazareth, where he had grown up. On the Sabbath day he went to the synagogue, as he always did, and stood up to read. The book of Isaiah the prophet was given to him. He opened the book and found the place where this is written:

> "The Lord has put his Spirit in me,
>   because he appointed me to tell the Good News to the poor.
> He has sent me to tell the captives they are free
>   and to tell the blind that they can see again. (Isaiah 61:1)
> God sent me to free those who have been treated unfairly (Isaiah 58:6)
> and to announce the time when the Lord will show his kindness."
> (Isaiah 61:2)

Divorce

Matthew 5:31-32 "It was also said, 'Anyone who divorces his wife must give her a written divorce paper.' But I tell you that anyone who divorces his wife forces her to be guilty of adultery. The only reason for a man to divorce his wife is if she has sexual relations with another man. And anyone who marries that divorced woman is guilty of adultery."

Matthew 19:8-9 Jesus answered, "Moses allowed you to divorce your wives because you refused to accept God's teaching, but divorce was not allowed in the beginning. I tell you that anyone who divorces his wife and marries another woman is guilty of adultery. The only reason for a man to divorce his wife is if his wife has sexual relations with another man."

Mark 10:5-10 Jesus said, "Moses wrote that command for you because you were stubborn. But when God made the world, 'he made them male and female.' 'So a man will leave his father and mother and be united with his wife, and the two will become one body.' So there are not two, but one. God has joined the two together, so no one should separate them."

Later, in the house, his followers asked Jesus again about the question of divorce. He answered, "Anyone who divorces his wife and marries another woman is guilty of adultery against her. And the woman who divorces her husband and marries another man is also guilty of adultery."

Luke 16:18 "If a man divorces his wife and marries another woman, he is guilty of adultery, and the man who marries a divorced woman is also guilty of adultery."

I Corinthians 7:10-16 Now I give this command for the married people. (The command is not from me; it is from the Lord.) A wife should not leave her husband. But is she does leave, she must not marry again, or she should make up with her husband. Also the husband should not divorce his wife.

For all the others I say this (I am saying this, not the Lord): If a Christian man has a wife who is not a believer, and she is happy to live with him, he must not divorce her. And if a Christian woman has a husband who is not a believer, and he is happy to live with her, she must not divorce him. The husband who is not a believer is made holy through his believing wife. And the wife who is not a believer is made holy through her believing husband. If this were not true, your children would not be clean, but now your children are holy.

But if those who are not believers decide to leave, let them leave. When this happens, the Christian man or woman is free. But God called us to live in peace.

Wife, you don't know; maybe you will save your husband. And husband, you don't know; maybe you will save your wife.

Most Important Rule

Matthew 7:12 "Do to others what you want them to do to you. This is the meaning of the law of Moses and the teaching of the prophets."

Mark 12:28-31 One of the teachers of the law came and heard Jesus arguing with the Sadducees. Seeing that Jesus gave good answers to their questions, he asked Jesus, "Which of the commands is most important?"

Jesus answered, "The most important command is this: 'Listen, people of Israel! The Lord our God is the only Lord. Love the Lord your God with all your heart, all your soul, all your mind, and all your strength.' The second command is this: 'Love your neighbor as you love yourself.' There are no commands more important than these."

Luke 10:25-37 Then an expert on the law stood up to test Jesus, saying, "Teacher, what must I do to get life forever?"

Jesus said, "What is written in the law? What do you read there?"

The man answered, "Love the Lord your God with all your heart, all your soul, all your strength, and all your mind." Also, "Love your neighbor as you love yourself."

Jesus said to him, "Your answer is right. Do this and you will live."

But the man, wanting to show the importance of his question, said to Jesus, "And who is my neighbor?"

Jesus answered, "As a man was going down from Jerusalem to Jericho, some robbers attacked him. They tore off his clothes, beat him, and left him lying there, almost dead. It happened that a Jewish priest was going down that road. When he saw the man, he walked by on the other side. Next, a Levite came there, and after he went over and looked at the man, he walked by on the other side of the road. Then a Samaritan traveling down the road came to where the hurt man was. When he saw the man, he felt very sorry for him. The Samaritan went to him, poured olive oil and wine on his wounds, and bandaged them. Then he put the hurt man on his own donkey and took him to an inn where he cared for him. The next day, the Samaritan brought out two coins, gave them to the innkeeper, and said, 'Take care of this man. If you spend more money on him, I will pay it back to you when I come again.'"

Then Jesus said, "Which one of these three men do you think was a neighbor to the man who was attacked by robbers?"

The expert on the law answered, "The one who showed him mercy."

Jesus said to him, "Then go and do what he did."

Fruits Of The Tree And False Prophets

Matthew 7:15-23 "Be careful of false prophets. They come to you looking gently like sheep, but they are really dangerous like wolves. You will know these people by what they do. Grapes don't come from thornbushes, and figs don't come from thorny weeds. In the same way, every good tree produces good fruit, but a bad tree produces bad fruit. A good tree cannot produce bad fruit, and a bad tree cannot produce good fruit. Every tree that does not produce good fruit is cut down and thrown into the fire. In the same way, you will know these false prophets by what they do.

"Not all those who say that I am their Lord will enter the kingdom of heaven. The only people who will enter the kingdom of heaven are those who do what my Father in heaven wants. On the last day many people will say to me, 'Lord, Lord, we spoke for you, and through you we forced out demons and did many miracles.' Then I will tell them clearly, 'Get away from me, you who do evil. I never knew you.'"

Matthew 12:33-37 "If you want good fruit, you must make the tree good. If your tree is not good, it will have bad fruit. A tree is known by the kind of fruit it produces. You snakes! You are evil people, so how can you say anything good? The mouth speaks the things that are in the heart. Good people have good things in their hearts, and so they say good things. But evil people have evil in their hearts, so they say evil things. And I tell you that on the Judgment Day people will be responsible for every careless thing they have said. The words you have said will be used to judge you. Some of your words will prove you right, but some of your words will prove you guilty."

I John 4:1-6 My dear friends, many false prophets have gone out into the world. So do not believe every spirit, but test the spirits to see if they are from God. This is how you can know God's Spirit: Every spirit who confesses that Jesus Christ came to earth as a human is from God. And every spirit who refuses to say this about Jesus is not from God. It is the sprit of the enemy of Christ, which you have heard is coming, and now he is already in the world.

My dear children, you belong to God and have defeated them; because God's Spirit, who is in you, is greater than the devil, who is in the world. And they belong to the world, so what they say is from the world, and the world listens to them. But we belong to God, and those who know God listen to us. But those who are not from God do not listen to us. That is how we know the Spirit that is true and the spirit that is false.

2 John 7-11 Many false teachers are in the world now who do not confess that Jesus Christ came to earth as a human. Anyone who does not confess this is a false teacher and an enemy of Christ. Be careful yourselves that you do not lose everything you have worked for. But that you receive your full reward.

Anyone who goes beyond Christ's teaching and does not continue to follow only his teaching does not have God. But whoever continues to follow the teaching of Christ has both the Father and the Son. If someone comes to you and does not bring this teaching, do not welcome or accept that person into your house. If you welcome such a person, you share in the evil work.

Luke 6:43-45 "A good tree does not produce bad fruit, nor does a bad tree produce good fruit. Each tree is known by its own fruit. People don't gather figs from thorn bushes, and they don't get grapes from bushes. Good people bring good things out of the good they stored in their hearts. But evil people bring evil things out of the evil they stored in their hearts. People speak the things that are in their hearts."

Luke 13:6-9 Jesus told this story: "A man had a fig tree planted in his vineyard. He came looking for some fruit on the tree, but he found none. So the man said to his gardener, 'I have been looking for fruit on this tree for three years, but I never find any. Cut it down. Why should it waste the ground?' But the servant answered, 'Master, let the tree have one more year to produce fruit. Let me dig up the dirt around it and put on some fertilizer. If the tree produces fruit next year, good. But if not, you can cut it down.'"

John 15:1-11 "I am the true vine; my Father is the gardener. He cuts off every branch of mine that does not produce fruit. And he trims and cleans every branch that produces fruit so that it will produce even more fruit. You are already clean because of the words I have spoken to you. Remain in me, and I will remain in you. A branch cannot produce fruit alone but must remain in the vine. In the same way, you cannot produce fruit alone but must remain in me.

"I am the vine, and you are the branches. If any remain in me and I remain in them, they produce much fruit. But without me they can do nothing. If any do not remain in me, they are like a branch that is thrown away and then dies. People pick up dead branches, throw them into the fire, and burn them. If you remain in me and follow my teachings, you can ask anything you want, and it will be given to you. You should produce much fruit and show that you are my followers, which brings glory to my Father. I loved you as the Father loved me. Now remain in my love. I have obeyed my Father's commands, and I remain in his love. In the same way, if you obey my commands, you will remain in my love. I have told you these things so that you can have the same joy I have and so that your joy will be the fullest possible joy."

Believing Is Obeying

Matthew 7:24-27 "Everyone who hears my words and obeys them is like a wise man who built his house on rock. It rained hard, the floods came, and the winds blew and hit that house. But it did not fall, because it was built on rock. Everyone who hears my words and does not obey them is like a foolish man who built his house on sand. It rained hard, the floods came, and the winds blew and hit that house, and it fell with a big crash."

Luke 6:46-49 Same as above with variations.

1 John 5:1-5 Everyone who believes that Jesus is the Christ is God's child, and whoever loves the Father also loves the Father's children. This is how we know we love God's children: when we love God and obey his commands. Loving God means obeying his commands. And God's commands are not too hard for us, because everyone who is a child of God conquers the world. And this is the victory that conquers the world—our faith. So the one who wins against the world is the person who believes that Jesus is the Son of God.

Fear God Not Humans

Matthew 10:28-31 "Don't be afraid of people, who can kill the body but cannot kill the soul. The only one you should fear is the one who can destroy the soul and the body in hell. Two sparrows cost only a penny, but not even one of them can die without your Father's knowing it. God even knows how many hairs are on your head. So don't be afraid. You are worth much more than many sparrows."

Philippians 2:12-13 My dear friends, you have always obeyed God when I was with you. It is even more important that you obey now while I am away from you. Keep on working to complete your salvation with fear and trembling, because God is working in you to help you want to do and be able to do what pleases him.

The Mission Of God Through Jesus

John 13:1-17 It was almost time for the Jewish Passover Feast. Jesus knew that it was time for him to leave this world and go back to the Father. He had always loved those who were his own in the world, and he loved them all the way to the end.

Jesus and his followers were at the evening meal. The devil had already persuaded Judas Iscariot, the son of Simon, to turn against Jesus. Jesus knew that the Father had given him power over everything and that he had come from God and was going back to God. So during the meal Jesus stood up and took off his outer clothing. Taking a towel, he wrapped it around his waist. Then he poured water into a bowl and began to wash the followers' feet, drying them with the towel that was wrapped around him.

Jesus came to Simon Peter, who said to him, "Lord, are you going to wash my feet?"

Jesus answered, "You don't understand now what I am doing, but you will understand later."

Peter said, "No, you will never wash my feet."

Jesus answered, "If I don't wash your feet, you are not one of my people."

Simon Peter answered, "Lord, then wash not only my feet, but wash my hands and my head, too!"

Jesus said, "After a person has had a bath, his whole body is clean. He needs only to wash his feet. And you men are clean, but not all of you." Jesus knew who would turn against him, and that is why he said, "Not all of you are clean."

When he had finished washing their feet, he put on his clothes and sat down again. He asked, "Do you understand what I have just done for you? You call me 'Teacher' and 'Lord,' and you are right, because that is what I am. If I, your Lord and Teacher, have washed your feet, you also should wash each other's feet. I did this as an example so that you should do as I have done for you. I tell you the truth, a servant is not greater than his master. A messenger is not greater than the one who sent him. If you know these things, you will be happy if you do them."

[Jesus washes his followers' feet. Jesus poured water (blood) into a bowl and began to wash the followers' feet. Jesus removes dirt (guilt). The Holy One gets down on his knees to remove our guilt. Jesus laid aside his glory and took the form of a servant. We also should wash each others' feet, (not God's feet, but others).]

Unforgivable Sin

Matthew 12:31-32 "So I tell you, people can be forgiven for every sin and everything they say against God. But whoever speaks against the Holy Spirit will not be forgiven. Anyone who speaks against the Son of Man can be forgiven, but anyone who speaks against the Holy Spirit will not be forgiven, now or in the future."

Mark 3:28-30 "I tell you're the truth, all sins that people do and all the things people say against God can be forgiven. But anyone who speaks against the Holy Spirit will never be forgiven; he is guilty of a sin that continues forever."

Jesus said this because the teachers of the law said that he had an evil spirit inside him.

Luke 12:10 "Anyone who speaks against the Son of Man can be forgiven, but anyone who speaks against the Holy Spirit will not be forgiven."

Luke 14:34-35 "Salt is good, but if it loses its salty taste, you cannot make it salty again. It is no good for the soil or for manure; it is thrown away.

"You people who can hear me, listen."

Hebrews 6:4-6 Some people cannot be brought back again to a changed life. They were once in God's light, and enjoyed heaven's gift, and shared in the Holy Spirit. They found out how good God's word is, and they received the powers of his new world. But they fell away from Christ. It is impossible to bring them back to a changed life again, because they are nailing the Son of God to a cross again and are shaming him in front of others.

Hebrews 10:26-31 If we decide to go on sinning after we have learned the truth, there is no longer any sacrifice for sins. There is nothing but fear in waiting for the judgment and the terrible fire that will destroy all those who live against God. Anyone who refused to obey the law of Moses was found guilty from the proof given by two or three witnesses. He was put to death without mercy. So what do you think should be done to those who do not respect the Son of God, who look at the blood of the agreement that made them holy as no different from others' blood, who insult the Spirit of God's grace? Surely they should have a much worse punishment. We know that God said, "I will punish those who do wrong; I will repay them." And he also said, "The Lord will judge his people." It is a terrible thing to fall into the hands of the living God.

2 Peter 2:20-22 They were made free from the evil in the world by knowing our Lord and Savior Jesus Christ. But if they return to evil things and those things control them, then it is worse for them than it was before. Yes, it would be better for them to have never known the right way than to know it and to turn away from the holy teaching that was given to them. What they did is like this true saying: "A dog goes back to what it has thrown up," and, "After a pig is washed, it goes back and rolls in the mud."

People Who Want More Proof: Miracles

Matthew 12:38-42 Then some of the Pharisees and teachers of the law answered Jesus, saying, "Teacher, we want to see you work a miracle as a sign."

Jesus answered, "Evil and sinful people are the ones who want to see a miracle for a sign. But no sign will be given to them, except the sign of the prophet Jonah. Jonah was in the stomach of the big fish for three days and three nights. In the same way, the Son of Man will be in the grave three days and three nights. On the Judgment Day the people from Nineveh will stand up with you people who live now, and they will show that you are guilty. When Jonah preached to them, they were sorry and changed their lives. And I tell you that someone greater than Jonah is here. On the Judgment Day, the Queen of the South will stand up with you people who live today. She will show that you are guilty, because she came from far away to listen to Solomon's wise teaching. And I tell you that someone greater than Solomon is here."

Luke 11:29-32 Same as above with variations.

Matthew 16:1-4 The Pharisees and Sadducees came to Jesus, wanting to trick him. So they asked him to show them a miracle from God.

Jesus answered, "At sunset you say we will have good weather, because the sky is red. And in the morning you say that it will be a rainy day, because the sky is dark and red. You see these signs in the sky and know what they mean. In the same way, you see the things that I am doing now, but you don't know their meaning. Evil and sinful people ask for a miracle as a sign, but they will not be given any sign, except the sign of Jonah." Then Jesus left them and went away.

Mark 8:11-13 Same as above with variations.

Matthew 26:67-68 Then the people there spat in Jesus' face and beat him with their fists. Others slapped him. They said, "Prove to us that you are a prophet, you Christ! Tell us who hit you!"

Luke 22:63-65 The men who were guarding Jesus began making fun of him and beating him.

They blindfolded him and said, "Prove that you are a prophet, and tell us who hit you." They said many cruel things to Jesus.

Luke 23:8-12 When Herod saw Jesus, he was very glad, because he had heard about Jesus and had wanted to meet him for a long time. He was hoping to see Jesus work a miracle. Herod asked Jesus many questions, but Jesus said nothing. The leading priests and teachers of the law were standing there, strongly accusing Jesus. After Herod and his soldiers had made fun of Jesus, they dressed him in a kingly robe and sent him back to Pilate. In the past, Pilate and Herod had always been enemies, but on that day they became friends.

1 Corinthians 1:22 The Jews ask for miracles, and the Greeks want wisdom. But we preach a crucified Christ. This is a big problem to the Jews, and it is foolishness to those who are not Jews.

Even With Miracles, Some Won't Believe

John 12: 37-43 Though Jesus had done many miracles in front of the people, they still did not believe in him. This was to bring about what Isaiah the prophet had said:

"Lord, who believed what we told them?

Who saw the Lord's power in this?" (Isaiah 53:1)

This is why the people could not believe: Isaiah also had said,

"He has blinded their eyes,

and he has closed their minds.

Otherwise they would see with their eyes

and understand in their minds

and come back to me and be healed." (Isaiah 6:10)

Isaiah said this because he saw Jesus' glory and spoke about him.

But many believed in Jesus, even many of the leaders. But because of the Pharisees, they did not say they believed in him for fear they would be put out of the synagogue. They loved praise from people more than praise from God.

Luke 16:19-31 (The Rich man and Lazarus) Jesus said, "There was a rich man who always dressed in the finest clothes and lived in luxury every day. And a very poor man named Lazarus, whose body was covered with sores, was laid at the rich man's gate. He wanted to eat only the small pieces of food that fell from the rich man's table. And the dogs would come and lick his sores. Later, Lazarus died, and the angels carried him to the arms of Abraham. The rich man died, too, and was buried. In the place of the dead, he was in much pain. The rich man saw Abraham far away with Lazarus at his side. He called, 'Father Abraham, have mercy on me! Send Lazarus to dip his finger in water and cool my tongue, because I am suffering in this fire!' But Abraham said, 'Child, remember when you were alive you had the good things in life, but bad things happened to Lazarus. Now he is comforted here, and you are suffering. Besides, there is a big pit between you and us, so no one can cross over to you, and no one can leave there and come here.' The rich man said, 'Father, then please send Lazarus to my father's house. I have five brothers, and Lazarus could warn them so that they will not come to this place of pain.' But Abraham said, 'They have the law of Moses and the writings of the prophets; let them learn from them.' The rich man said, 'No, father Abraham! **If someone goes to them from the dead, they would believe and change their hearts and lives.' But Abraham said to him, 'If they will not listen to Moses and the prophets, they will not listen to someone who comes back from the dead.'"**

Stories Used By Jesus

Matthew 13:1-23 (The story about planting seed/Why Jesus used stories to teach)... The followers came to Jesus and asked, "Why do you use stories to teach the people?"

Jesus answered, "You have been chosen to know the secrets about the kingdom of heaven, but others cannot know these secrets. Those who have understanding will be given more, and they will have all they need. But those who do not have understanding, even what they have will be taken away from them. This is why I use stories to teach the people: They see, but they don't really see. They hear, but they don't really hear or understand. So they show that the things Isaiah said about them are true:

'You will listen and listen, but you will not understand.
You will look and look, but you will not learn.
For the minds of these people have become stubborn.
They do not hear with their ears,
and they have closed their eyes.
Otherwise they might really understand
what they see with their eyes
and hear with their ears.
They might really understand in their minds
and come back to me and be healed.' (Isaiah 6:9-10)

But you are blessed, because you see with your eyes and hear with your ears. I tell you the truth, many prophets and good people wanted to see the things that you now see, but they did not see them. And they wanted to hear the things that you now hear, but they did not hear them.

"So listen to the meaning of that story about the farmer. What is the seed that fell by the road? That seed is like the person who hears the message about the kingdom but does not understand it. The Evil One comes and takes away what was planted in that person's heart. And what is the seed that fell on rocky ground? That seed is like the person who hears the teaching and quickly accepts it with joy. But he does not let the teaching go deep into his life, so he keeps it only a short time. When trouble or persecution comes because of the teaching he accepted, he quickly gives up. And what is the seed that fell among the thorny weeds? That seed is like the person who hears the teaching but lets worries about this life and the temptation of wealth stop that teaching from growing. So the teaching does not produce fruit in that person's life. But what is the seed that fell on the good ground? That seed is like the person who hears the teaching and understands it. That person grows and produces fruit, sometimes a hundred times more, sometimes sixty times more, and sometimes thirty times more."

Mark 4:1-20 Same as above with variations.
Luke 8:4-15 Same as above with variations.

Matthew 13:24-30 (A story about wheat and weeds) Then Jesus told them another story: "The kingdom of heaven is like a man who planted good seed in his field. That night, when everyone was asleep, his enemy came and planted weeds among the wheat and then left. Later, the wheat sprouted and the heads of grain grew, but the weeds also grew. Then the man's servants came to him and said, 'You planted good seed in your field. Where did the weeds come from?' The man answered, 'An enemy planted weeds.' The servants asked, 'Do you want us to pull up the weeds?' The man answered, 'No, because when you pull up the weeds, you might also pull up the wheat. Let the weeds and the wheat grow together until the harvest time. At harvest time I will tell the workers, "First gather the weeds and tie them together to be burned. Then gather the wheat and bring it to my barn."'"

Matthew 13:31-35 (Stories of mustard seed and yeast) Then Jesus told another story: "The kingdom of heaven is like a mustard seed that a man planted in is field. That seed is the smallest of all seeds, but when it grows, it is one of the largest garden plants. It becomes big enough for the wild birds to come and build nests in its branches."

Then Jesus told another story: "The kingdom of heaven is like yeast that a woman took and hid in a large tub of flour until it made all the dough rise."

Jesus used stories to tell all these things to the people; he always used stories to teach them. This is as the prophet said:

> "I will speak using stories;
> I will tell things that have been secret since the
> world was made." (Psalm 78:2)

Mark 4:30-34 Same as above with variations.
Luke 13:18-21 Same as above with variations.

Mark 4:26-29 Then Jesus said, "The kingdom of God is like someone who plants seed in the ground. Night and day, whether the person is asleep or awake, the seed still grows, but the person does not know how it grows. By itself the earth produces grain. First the plant grows, then the head, and then all the grain in the head. When the grain is ready, the farmer cuts it, because this is the harvest time."

Matthew 13:44-46 "The kingdom of heaven is like a treasure hidden in a field. One day a man found the treasure, and then he hid it in the field again. He was so happy that he went and sold everything he owned to buy that field.

"Also, the kingdom of heaven is like a man looking for fine pearls. When he found a very valuable pearl, he went and sold everything he had and bought it."

Matthew 13:47-52 "Also, the kingdom of heaven is like a net that was put into the lake and caught many different kinds of fish. When it was full, the fishermen pulled the net to the shore. They sat down and put all the good fish in baskets and threw away the bad fish. It will be this way at the end of the world. The angels will come and separate the evil people from the good people. The angels will throw the evil people into the blazing furnace, where people will cry and grind their teeth with pain."

Jesus asked his followers, "Do you understand all these things?"

They answered, "Yes, we understand."

Then Jesus said to them, "So every teacher of the law who has been taught about the kingdom of heaven is like the owner of a house. He brings out both new things and old things he has saved."

Mark 12:1-12 Jesus began to use stories to teach the people. He said, "A man planted a vineyard. He put a wall around it and dug a hole for a winepress and built a tower. Then he leased the land to some farmers and left for a trip. When it was time for the grapes to be picked, he sent a servant to the farmers to get his share of the grapes. But the farmers grabbed the servant and beat him and sent him away empty-handed. Then the man sent another servant. They hit him on the head and showed no respect for him. So the man sent another servant, whom they killed. The man sent many other servants; the farmers beat some of them and killed others.

"The man had one person left to send, his son whom he loved. He sent him last of all, saying, 'They will respect my son.'

But the farmers said to each other, 'This son will inherit the vineyard. If we kill him, it will be ours.' So they took the son, killed him, and threw him out of the vineyard.

"So what will the owner of the vineyard do? He will come and kill those farmers and will give the vineyard to other farmers. Surely you have read this Scripture:

'The stone that the builders rejected
    became the cornerstone.
The Lord did this,
    and it is wonderful to us.'" (Psalm 118:22-23)

The Jewish leaders knew that the story was about them. So they wanted to find a way to arrest Jesus, but they were afraid of the people. So the leaders left him and went away.

Luke 20:9-19 Same as above with variations.
Matthew 21:33-46 Same as above with variations.

Luke 15:11-32 (The story about the prodigal son) Then Jesus said, "A man had two sons. The younger son said to his father, 'Give me my share of the property.' So the father divided the property between his two sons. Then the younger son gathered up all that was his and traveled far away to another country. There he wasted his money in foolish living. After he had spent everything, a time came when there was no food anywhere in the country, and the son was poor and hungry. So he got a job with one of the citizens there who sent the son into the fields to feed pigs. The son was so hungry that he wanted to eat the pods the pigs were eating, but no one gave him anything. When he realized what he was doing, he thought, 'All of my father's servants have plenty of food. But I am here, almost dying with hunger. I will leave and return to my father and say to him, "Father, I have sinned against God and have done wrong to you. I am no longer worthy to be called your son, but let me be like one of your servants."' So the son left and went to his father.

"While the son was still a long way off, his father saw him and felt sorry for his son. So the father ran to him and hugged and kissed him. The son said, 'Father, I have sinned against God and have done wrong to you. I am no longer worthy to be called your son.' But the father said to his servants, 'Hurry! Bring the best clothes and put them on him. Also, put a ring on his finger and sandals on his feet. And get our fat calf and kill it so we can have a feast and celebrate. My son was dead, but now he is alive again! He was lost, but now he is found!' So they began to celebrate.

"The older son was in the field, and as he came closer to the house, he heard the sound of music and dancing. So he called to one of the servants and asked what all this meant. The servant said, 'Your brother has come back, and your father killed the fat calf, because your brother came home safely.' The older son was angry and would not go in to the feast. So his father went out and begged him to come in. But the older son said to his father, 'I have served you like a slave for many years and have always obeyed your commands. But you never gave me even a young goat to have at a feast with my friends. But your other son, who wasted all your money on prostitutes, comes home, and you kill the fat calf for him!' The father said to him, 'Son, you are always with me, and all that I have is yours. We had to celebrate and be happy because your brother was dead, but now he is alive. He was lost, but now he is found.'"

Matthew 21:28-32 "Tell me what you think about this: A man had two sons. He went to the first son and said, 'Son, go and work today in my vineyard.' The son answered, 'I will not go.' But later the son changed his mind and went. Then the father went to the other son and said, 'Son, go and work today in my vineyard.' The son answered, 'Yes, sir, I will go and work,' but he did not go. Which of the two sons obeyed his father?"

The priests and leaders answered, "The first son."

Jesus said to them, "I tell you the truth, the tax collectors and the prostitutes will enter the kingdom of God before you do. John came to show you the right way to live. You did not believe him, but the tax collectors and prostitutes believed him. Even after seeing this, you still refused to change your ways and believe him."

Luke 12:15-21 Then Jesus said to them, "Be careful and guard against all kinds of greed. Life is not measured by how much one owns."

Then Jesus told this story: "There was a rich man who had some land, which grew a good crop. He thought to himself, 'What will I do? I have no place to keep all my crops.' Then he said, 'This is what I will do: I will tear down my barns and build bigger ones, and there I will store all my grain and other goods. Then I can say to myself, "I have enough good things stored to last for many years. Rest, eat, drink, and enjoy life!"'

"But God said to him, 'Foolish man! Tonight your life will be taken from you. So who will get those things you have prepared for yourself?'

"This is how it will be for those who store up things for themselves and are not rich toward God."

Luke 16:19-31 (The story about the rich man and Lazarus) Jesus said, "There was a rich man who always dressed in the finest clothes and lived in luxury every day. And a very poor man named Lazarus, whose body was covered with sores, was laid at the rich man's gate. He wanted to eat only the small pieces of food that fell from the rich man's table. And the dogs would come and lick his sores. Later, Lazarus died, and the angels carried him to the arms of Abraham. The rich man died, too, and was buried. In the place of the dead, he was in much pain. The rich man saw Abraham far away with Lazarus at his side. He called, 'Father Abraham, have mercy on me! Send Lazarus to dip his finger in water and cool my tongue, because I am suffering in this fire!' But Abraham said, 'Child, remember when you were alive you had the good things in life, but bad things happened to Lazarus. Now he is comforted here, and you are suffering. Besides, there is a big pit between you and us, so no one can cross over to you, and no one can leave there and come here.' The rich man said, 'Father, then please send Lazarus to my father's house. I have five brothers, and Lazarus could warn them so that they will not come to this place of pain.' But

Abraham said, 'They have the law of Moses and the writings of the prophets; let them learn from them.' The rich man said, 'No, father Abraham! If someone goes to them from the dead, they would believe and change their hearts and lives.' But Abraham said to him, 'If they will not listen to Moses and the prophets, they will not listen to someone who comes back from the dead.'"

Matthew 18:23-35 "The kingdom of heaven is like a king who decided to collect the money his servants owed him. When the king began to collect his money, a servant who owed him several million dollars was brought to him. But the servant did not have enough money to pay his master, the king. So the master ordered that everything the servant owned should be sold, even the servant's wife and children. Then the money would be used to pay the king what the servant owed.

"But the servant fell on his knees and begged, 'Be patient with me, and I will pay you everything I owe.' The master felt sorry for his servant and told him he did not have to pay it back. Then he let the servant go free.

"Later, that same servant found another servant who owed him a few dollars. The servant grabbed him around the neck and said, 'Pay me the money you owe me!'

"The other servant fell on his knees and begged him, 'Be patient with me, and I will pay you everything I owe.'

"But the first servant refused to be patient. He threw the other servant into prison until he could pay everything he owed. When the other servants saw what had happened, they were very sorry. So they went and told their master all that had happened.

"Then the master called his servant in and said, 'You evil servant! Because you begged me to forget what you owed, I told you that you did not have to pay anything. You should have showed mercy to that other servant, just as I showed mercy to you.' The master was very angry and put the servant in prison to be punished until he could pay everything he owed.

"This king did what my heavenly Father will do to you if you do not forgive your brother or sister from your heart."

Luke 15:1-10 (A lost sheep, a lost coin) The tax collectors and sinners all came to listen to Jesus. But the Pharisees and the teachers of the law began to complain: "Look, this man welcomes sinners and even eats with them."

Then Jesus told them this story: "Suppose one of you has a hundred sheep but loses one of them. Then he will leave the other ninety-nine sheep in the open field and go out and look for the lost sheep until he finds it. And when he finds it, he happily puts it on his shoulders and goes home. He calls to his friends and neighbors and says, 'Be happy with me because I found my lost sheep.' In the same way, I tell you there is more joy in heaven over one sinner who changes his heart and life, than over ninety-nine good people who don't need to change.

"Suppose a woman has ten silver coins, but loses one. She will light a lamp, sweep the house, and look carefully for the coin until she finds it. And when she finds it, she will call her friends and neighbors and say, 'Be happy with me because I have found the coin that I lost.' In the same way, there is joy in the presence of the angels of God when one sinner changes his heart and life."

Luke 16:1-13 (True wealth) Jesus also said to his followers, "Once there was a rich man who had a manager to take care of his business. This manager was accused of cheating him. So he called the manager in and said to him, 'What is this I hear about you? Give me a report of what you have done with my money, because you can't be my manager any longer.' The manager thought to himself, 'What will I do since my master is taking my job away from me? I am not strong enough to dig ditches, and I am ashamed to beg. I know what I'll do so that when I lose my job people will welcome me into their homes.'

"So the manager called in everyone who owed the master any money. He asked the first one, 'How much do you owe?' He answered, 'Eight hundred gallons of olive oil.' The manager said to him, 'Take your bill, sit down quickly, and write four hundred gallons.' Then the manager asked another one, 'How much do you owe?' He answered, 'One thousand bushels of wheat.' Then the manager said to him, 'Take your bill and write eight hundred bushels.' So, the master praised the dishonest manager for being smart. Yes, worldly people are smarter with their own kind than spiritual people are.

"I tell you, make friends for yourselves using worldly riches so that when those riches are gone, you will be welcomed in those homes that continue forever. Whoever can be trusted with a little can also be trusted with a lot, and whoever is dishonest with a little is dishonest with a lot. If you cannot be trusted with worldly riches, then who will trust you with true riches? And if you cannot be trusted with things that belong to someone else, who will give you things of your own?

"No servant can serve two masters. The servant will hate one master and love the other, or will follow one master and refuse to follow the other. You cannot serve both God and worldly riches."

God's Law Versus Human Rules

Matthew 15:1-11 Then some Pharisees and teachers of the law came to Jesus from Jerusalem. They asked him, "Why don't your followers obey the unwritten laws which have been handed down to us? They don't wash their hands before they eat."

Jesus answered, "And why do you refuse to obey God's command so that you can follow your own teachings? God said, 'Honor your father and your mother,' and 'anyone who says cruel things to his father or mother must be put to death.' But you say a person can tell his father or mother, 'I have something I could use to help you, but I have given it to God already.' You teach that person not to honor his father or his mother. You rejected what God said for the sake of your own rules. You are hypocrites! Isaiah was right when he said about you:

'These people show honor to me with words,
> but their hearts are far from me.

Their worship of me is worthless.
> The things they teach are nothing but human rules.'" (Isaiah 29:13)

After Jesus called the crowd to him he said, "Listen and understand what I am saying. It is not what people put into their mouths that make them unclean. It is what comes out of their mouths that makes them unclean."

Mark 7:5-13 Same as above with variations.

Luke 13:14-17 (Jesus is criticized for healing on the Sabbath day) **The synagogue leader was angry because Jesus healed on the Sabbath day. He said to the people, "There are six days when one has to work. So come to be healed on one of those days, and not on the Sabbath day."**

The Lord answered, "You hypocrites! Doesn't each of you untie your work animals and lead them to drink water every day—even on the Sabbath day? This woman that I healed, a daughter of Abraham, has been held by Satan for eighteen years. Surely it is not wrong for her to be freed from her sickness on a Sabbath day!" When Jesus said this, all of those who were criticizing him were ashamed, but the entire crowd rejoiced at all the wonderful things Jesus was doing.

Luke 14:1-6 On a Sabbath day, when Jesus went to eat at the home of a leading Pharisee, the people were watching Jesus very closely. And in front of him was a man with dropsy. Jesus said to the Pharisees and experts on the law, "Is it right or wrong to heal on the Sabbath day?" But they would not answer his question. So Jesus took the man, healed him, and sent him away. Jesus said to the Pharisee and teachers of the law, "If your child or ox falls into a well on the Sabbath day, will you not pull him out quickly?" And they could not answer him.

Colossians 2:16-23 So do not let anyone make rules for you about eating and drinking or about a religious feast, a New Moon Festival, or a Sabbath day. These things were like a shadow of what was to come. But what is true and real has come and is found in Christ. Do not let anyone disqualify you by making you humiliate yourself and worship angels. Such people enter into visions, which fill them with foolish pride because of their human way of thinking. They do not hold tightly to Christ, the head. It is from him that all the parts of the body are cared for and held together. So it grows in the way God wants it to grow.

Since you died with Christ and were made free from the ruling spirits of the world, why do you act as if you still belong to this world by following rules like these: "Don't eat this," "Don't taste that," "Don't even touch that thing"? These rules refer to earthy things that are gone as soon as they are used. They are only man-made commands and teachings. They seem to be wise, but they are only part of a man-made religion. They make people pretend not to be proud and make them punish their bodies, but they do not really control the evil desires of the sinful self.

Jesus Is The Christ

John 4:25-26 (Jacob's well and the Samaritan Woman) The woman said, "I know that the Messiah is coming." (Messiah is the One called Christ.) "When the Messiah comes, he will explain everything to us."

Then Jesus said, "I am he—I, the one talking to you."

John 4:42 They said to the woman, "First we believed in Jesus because of your speech, but now we believe because we heard him ourselves. We know that this man really is the Savior of the world."

Matthew 16:13-20 When Jesus came to the area of Caesarea Philippi, he asked his followers, "Who do people say the Son of Man is?"

They answered, "Some say you are John the Baptist. Others say you are Elijah, and still others say you are Jeremiah or one of the prophets."

Then Jesus asked them, "And who do you say I am?"

Simon Peter answered, "You are the Christ, the Son of the living God."

Jesus answered, "You are blessed, Simon son of Jonah, because no person taught you that. My Father in heaven showed you who I am. So I tell you, you are Peter. On this rock I will built my church, and the power of death will not be able to defeat it. I will give you the keys of the kingdom of heaven; the things you don't allow on earth will be the things that God does not allow, and the things you allow on earth will be the things that God allows." Then Jesus warned his followers not to tell anyone he was the Christ.

Mark 8:27-29 Same as above with variations.

Luke 9:18-20 Same as above with variations.

Matthew 26:63-64 Again the high priest said to Jesus, "I command you by the power of the living God: Tell us if you are the Christ, the Son of God."

Jesus answered, "Those are your words. But I tell you, in the future you will see the Son of Man sitting at the right hand of God, the Powerful One, and coming on clouds in the sky."

Mark 15:2 Same as above with variations.

Luke 23:1-5 Same as above with variations.

Luke 22:66-71 When day came, the council of the older leaders of the people, both the leading priests and the teachers of the law, came together and led Jesus to their highest court. They said, "If you are the Christ, tell us."

Jesus said to them, "If I tell you, you will not believe me. And if I ask you, you will not answer. But from now on, the Son of Man will sit at the right hand of the powerful God."

They all said, "Then are you the son of God?"

Jesus said to them, "You say that I am."

They said, "Why do we need witnesses now? We ourselves heard him say this."

Mark 14:61-62 But Jesus said nothing; he did not answer.

The high priest asked Jesus another question: "Are you the Christ, the Son of the blessed God?"

Jesus answered, "I am. And in the future you will see the Son of Man sitting at the right hand of God, the Powerful One, and coming on the clouds in the sky."

Mark 1:9-11 At that time Jesus came from the town of Nazareth in Galilee and was baptized by John in the Jordan River. Immediately, as Jesus was coming up out of the water, he saw heaven open. The Holy Spirit came down on him like a dove, and a voice came from heaven: "You are my Son, whom I love, and I am very pleased with you."

Matthew 3:16-17 Same as above with variations.

Luke 3:21-22 Same as above with variations.

Mark 1:23-24 Just then, a man was there in the synagogue who had an evil spirit in him. He shouted, "Jesus of Nazareth! What do you want with us? Did you come to destroy us? I know who you are—God's Holy One!"

Mark 9:37 "Whoever accepts a child like this in my name accepts me. And whoever accepts me accepts the One who sent me."

Luke 4:16-21 Jesus traveled to Nazareth, where he had grown up. On the Sabbath day he went to the synagogue, as he always did, and stood up to read. The book of Isaiah the prophet was given to him. He opened the book and found the place where this is written:

> "The Lord has put his Spirit in me,
>> because he appointed me to tell the Good News to the poor.
> He has sent me to tell the captives they are free
>> and to tell the blind that they can see again. (Isaiah 61:1)
> God sent me to free those who have been treated unfairly (Isaiah 58:6)
>> and to announce the time when the Lord will show his kindness."
> (Isaiah 61:2)

Jesus closed the book, gave it back to the assistant, and sat down. Everyone in the synagogue was watching Jesus closely. He began to say to them, "While you heard these words just now, they were coming true!"

John 7:25-29 Then some of the people who lived in Jerusalem said, "This is the man they are trying to kill. But he is teaching where everyone can see and hear him, and no one is trying to stop him. Maybe the leaders have decided he really is the Christ. But we know where this man is from. And when the real Christ comes, no one will know where he comes from."

Jesus, teaching in the Temple, cried out, "Yes, you know me, and you know where I am from. But I have not come by my own authority. I was sent by the One who is true, whom you don't know. But I know him, because I am from him, and he sent me."

John 7:41-44 Others said, "He is the Christ."

Still others said, "The Christ will not come from Galilee. The Scripture says that the Christ will come from David's family and from Bethlehem, the town where David lived." So the people did not agree with each other about Jesus. Some of them wanted to arrest him, but no one was able to touch him.

John 20:30-31 Jesus did many other miracles in the presence of his followers that are not written in this book. But these are written so that you may believe that Jesus is the Christ, the Son of God. Then, by believing, you may have life through his name.

I Timothy 2:3-6 This is good, and it pleases God our Savior, who wants all people to be saved and to know the truth. There is one God and one way human beings can reach God. That way is through Christ Jesus, who is himself human. He gave himself as a payment to free all people. He is proof that came at the right time.

John 18:37-38 Pilate said, "So you are a king!"

Jesus answered, "You are the one saying I am a king. This is why I was born and came into the world: to tell people the truth. And everyone who belongs to the truth listens to me."

John 9:35-39 When Jesus heard that they had thrown him out, Jesus found him and said, "Do you believe in the Son of Man?"

He asked, "Who is the Son of Man, sir, so that I can believe in him?"

Jesus said to him, "You have seen him. The Son of Man is the one talking with you."

He said, "Lord, I believe!" Then the man worshiped Jesus.

Jesus said, "I came into this world so that the world could be judged. I came so that the blind would see and so that those who see will become blind."

John 9:4 "While it is daytime, we must continue doing the work of the One who sent me. Night is coming, when no one can work."

Christians Are To Act Like This

Luke 9:23-27 Jesus said to all of them, "If people want to follow me, they must give up the things they want. They must be willing to give up their lives daily to follow me. Those who want to save their lives will give up true life. But those who give up their lives for me will have true life. It is worth nothing for them to have the whole world if they themselves are destroyed or lost. If people are ashamed of me and my teaching, then the Son of Man will be ashamed of them when he comes in his glory and with the glory of the Father and the holy angels. I tell you the truth, some people standing here will see the kingdom of God before they die."

Luke 9:46-48 Jesus' followers began to have an argument about which one of them was the greatest. Jesus knew what they were thinking, so he took a little child and stood the child beside him. Then Jesus said, "Whoever accepts this little child in my name accepts me. And whoever accepts me accepts the One who sent me, because whoever is least among you all is really the greatest."

Mark 9:33-37 Same as above with variations.

Matthew 25:35-46 "'I was hungry, and you gave me food. I was thirsty, and you gave me something to drink. I was alone and away from home, and you invited me into your house. I was without clothes, and your gave me something to wear. I was sick, and you cared for me. I was in prison, and you visited me.'

"Then the good people will answer, 'Lord, when did we see you hungry and give you food, or thirsty and give you something to drink? When did we see you alone and away from home and invite you into our house? When did we see you without clothes and give you something to wear? When did we see you sick or in prison and care for you?'

"Then the King will answer, 'I tell you the truth, anything you did for even the least of my people here, you also did for me.'

"Then the King will say to those on his left, 'Go away from me. You will be punished. Go into the fire that burns forever that was prepared for the devil and his angels. I was hungry, and you gave me nothing to eat. I was thirsty, and you gave me nothing to drink. I was alone and away from home, and you did not invite me into your house. I was without clothes, and you gave me nothing to wear. I was sick and in prison, and you did not care for me.'

"Then those people will answer, 'Lord, when did we see you hungry or thirsty or alone and away from home or without clothes or sick or in prison? When did we see these things and not help you?'

"Then the King will answer, 'I tell you the truth, anything you refused to do for even the least of my people here, you refused to do for me.'

"These people will go off to be punished forever, but the good people will go to live forever."

Matthew 18:1-9 At that time the followers came to Jesus and asked, "Who is greatest in the kingdom of heaven?"

Jesus called a little child to him and stood the child before his followers. Then he said, "I tell you the truth, you must change and become like little children. Otherwise, you will never enter the kingdom of heaven. The greatest person in the kingdom of heaven is the one who makes himself humble like this child.

"Whoever accepts a child in my name accepts me. If one of these little children believes in me, and someone causes that child to sin, it would be better for that person to have a large stone tied around the neck and be drowned in the sea. How terrible for the people of the world because of the things that cause them to sin. Such things will happen, but how terrible for the one who causes them to happen! If your hand or your foot causes you to sin, cut it off and throw it away. It is better for you to lose part of your body and live forever than to have two hands and two feet and be thrown into the fire that burns forever. If your eye causes you to sin, take it out and throw it away. It is better for you to have only one eye and live forever than to have two eyes and be thrown into the fire of hell."

Matthew 19:16-26 A man came to Jesus and asked, "Teacher, what good thing must I do to have life forever?"

Jesus answered, "Why do you ask me about what is good? Only God is good. But if you want to have life forever, obey the commands."

The man asked, "Which commands?"

Jesus answered, "'You must not murder anyone; you must not be guilty of adultery; you must not steal; you must not tell lies about your neighbor; honor your father and mother; and love your neighbor as you love yourself.'"

The young man said, "I have obeyed all these things. What else do I need to do?"

Jesus answered, "If you want to be perfect, then go and sell your possessions and give the money to the poor. If you do this, you will have treasure in heaven. Then come and follow me."

But when the young man heard this, he left sorrowfully, because he was rich.

Then Jesus said to his followers, "I tell you the truth, it will be hard for rich person to enter the kingdom of heaven. Yes, I tell you that it is easier for a camel to go through the eye of a needle than for a rich person to enter the kingdom of God."

When Jesus' followers heard this, they were very surprised and asked, "Then who can be saved?"

Jesus looked at them and said, "This is something people cannot do, but God can do all things."

Luke 18:18-24 Same as above with variations.

Mark 10:17-31 Same as above with variations.

Luke 6:20-26 Jesus looked at his followers and said,

>"You people who are poor are happy,
>   because the kingdom of God belongs to you.
>You people who are now hungry are happy,
>   because you will be satisfied.
>You people who are now crying are happy,
>   because you will laugh with joy.

"People will hate you, shut you out, insult you, and say you are evil because you follow the Son of Man. But when they do, you will be happy. Be full of joy at that time, because you have a great reward waiting for you in heaven. Their ancestors did the same things to the prophets.

>"But how terrible it will be for you who are rich,
>   because you have had your easy life.
>How terrible it will be for you who are full now,
>   because you will be hungry.
>How terrible it will be for you who are laughing now,
>   because you will be sad and cry.

"How terrible when everyone says only good things about you, because their ancestors said the same things about the false prophets."

Mark 10:42-45 Jesus called them together and said, "The non-Jewish people have rulers. You know that those rulers love to show their power over the people, and their important leaders love to use all their authority. But it should not be that way among you. Whoever wants to become great among you must serve the rest of you like a servant. Whoever wants to become the first among you must serve all of you like a slave. In the same way, the Son of Man did not come to be served. He came to serve others and to give his life as a ransom for many people."

Luke 22:24-27 Same as above with variations.

Luke 12:8-9 "I tell you, all those who stand before others and say they believe in me, I, the Son of Man, will say before the angels of God that they belong to me. But all who stand before others and say they do not believe in me, I will say before the angels of God that they do not belong to me."

Luke 12:22-34 Jesus said to his followers, "So I tell you, don't worry about the food you need to live, or about the clothes you need for your body. Life is more than food, and the body is more than clothes. Look at the birds. They don't plant or harvest, they don't have storerooms or barns, but God feeds them. And you are worth much more than birds. You cannot add any time to your life by worrying about it. If you cannot do even the little things, then why worry about the big things? Consider how the lilies grow; they don't work or make clothes for themselves. But I tell you that even Solomon with his riches was not dressed as beautifully as one of these flowers. God clothes the grass in the field, which is alive today but tomorrow is thrown into the fire. So how much more will God clothe you? Don't have so little faith! Don't always think about what you will eat or what you will drink, and don't keep worrying. All the people in the world are trying to get these things, and your Father knows you need them. But seek God's kingdom, and all the other things you need will be given to you.

"Don't fear, little flock, because your Father wants to give you the kingdom. Sell your possessions and give to the poor. Get for yourselves purses that will not wear out, the treasure in heaven that never runs out, where thieves can't steal and moths can't destroy. Your heart will be where your treasure is."

Matthew 6:25-34 Same as above with variations.

Matthew 6:34 So don't worry about tomorrow, because tomorrow will have its own worries. Each day has enough trouble of its own.

Luke 18:9-14 Jesus told this story to some people who thought they were very good and looked down on everyone else. "A Pharisee and a tax collector both went to the Temple to pray. The Pharisee stood alone and prayed, 'God, I thank you that I am not like other people who steal, cheat, or take part in adultery, or even like this tax collector. I give up eating twice a week, and I give one-tenth of everything I get!'

"The tax collector, standing at a distance, would not even look up to heaven. But he beat on his chest because he was so sad. He said, 'God, have mercy on me, a sinner.' It tell you, when this man went home, he was right with God, but the Pharisee was not. All who make themselves great will be made humble, but all who make themselves humble will be made great."

Luke 6:27-36 "But I say to you who are listening, love your enemies. Do good to those who hate you, bless those who curse you, pray for those who are cruel to you. If anyone slaps you on one cheek, offer him the other check, too. If someone takes your coat, do not stop him from taking your shirt. Give to everyone who asks you, and when someone takes something that is yours, don't ask for it back. Do to others what you would want them to do to you. If you love only the people who love you, what praise should you get? Even sinners love the people who love them. If you do good only to those who do good to you, what praise should you get? Even sinners do that! If you lend things to people, always hoping to get something back, what praise should you get? Even sinners lend to other sinners so they can get back the same amount! But love your enemies, do good to them, and lend to them without hoping to get anything back. Then you will have great reward, and you will be children of the Most High God, because he is kind even to people who are ungrateful and full of sin. Show mercy, just as your Father shows mercy."

Luke 6:37-42 "Don't judge other people, and you will not be judged. Don't accuse others of being guilty, and you will not be accused of being guilty. Forgive, and you will be forgiven. Give, and you will receive. You will be given much. Pressed down, shaken together, and running over, it will spill into your lap. The way you give to others is the way God will give to you."

Jesus told them this story: "Can a blind person lead another blind person? No! Both of them will fall into a ditch. A student is not better than the teacher, but the student who has been fully trained will be like the teacher.

"Why do you notice the little piece of dust in your friend's eye, but you don't notice the big piece of wood in your own eye? How can you say to your friend, 'Friend, let me take that little piece of dust out of your eye' when you cannot see that big piece of wood in your own eye! You hypocrite! First, take the wood out of your own eye. Then you will see clearly to take the dust out of your friend's eye."

Luke 10:25-37 (The Good Samaritan) Then an expert on the law stood up to test Jesus, saying, "Teacher, what must I do to get life forever?"

Jesus said, "What is written in the law? What do you read there?"

The man answered, "Love the Lord your God with all your heart, all your soul, all your strength, and all your mind." Also, "Love your neighbor as you love yourself."

Jesus said to him, "Your answer is right. Do this and you will live."

But the man, wanting to show the importance of his question, said to Jesus, "And who is my neighbor?"

Jesus answered, "As a man was going down from Jerusalem to Jericho, some robbers attacked him. They tore off his clothes, beat him, and left him lying there, almost dead. It happened that a Jewish priest was going down that road. When he saw the man, he walked by on the other side. Next, a Levite came there, and after he went over and looked at the man, he walked by on the other side of the road. Then a Samaritan traveling down the road came to where the hurt man was. When he saw the man, he felt very sorry for him. The Samaritan went to him, poured olive oil and wine on his wounds, and bandaged them. Then he put the hurt man on his own donkey and took him to an inn where he cared for him. The next day, the Samaritan brought out two coins, gave them to the innkeeper, and said, 'Take care of this man. If you spend more money on him, I will pay it back to you when I come again.'"

Then Jesus said, "Which one of these three men do you think was a neighbor to the man who was attacked by robbers?"

The expert on the law answered, "The one who showed him mercy."

Jesus said to him, "Then go and do what he did."

Luke 12:13-15 Someone in the crowd said to Jesus, "Teacher, tell my brother to divide with me the property our father left us."

But Jesus said to him, "Who said I should judge or decide between you?" Then Jesus said to them, "Be careful and guard against all kinds of greed. Life is not measured by how much one owns."

Luke 12:35-40 "Be dressed, ready for service, and have your lamps shining. Be like servants who are waiting for their master to come home from a wedding party. When he comes and knocks, the servants immediately open the door for him. They will be blessed when their master comes home, because he sees that they were watching for him. I tell you the truth, the master will dress himself to serve and tell the servants to sit a the table, and he will serve them. Those servants will be happy when he comes in and finds them still waiting, even if it is midnight or later.

"Remember this: If the owner of the house knew what time a thief was coming, he would not allow the thief to enter his house. So you also must be ready, because the Son of Man will come at a time when you don't expect him!"

Luke 14:7-11 When Jesus noticed that some of the guests were choosing the best places to sit, he told this story:

"When someone invites you to a wedding feast, don't take the most important seat, because someone more important than you may have been invited. The host, who invited both of you, will come to you and say, 'Give this person your seat.' Then you will be embarrassed and will have to move to the last place. So when you are invited, go sit in a seat that is not important. When the host comes to you, he may say, 'Friend, move up here to a more important place.' Then all the other guests will respect you. All who make themselves great will be made humble, but those who make themselves humble will be made great."

Luke 14:34-35 "Salt is good, but if it loses its salty taste, you cannot make it salty again. It is no good for the soil or for manure; it is thrown away.

"You people who can hear me, listen."

Luke 17:7-10 "Suppose one of you has a servant who has been plowing the ground or caring for the sheep. When the servant comes in from working in the field, would you say, 'Come in and sit down to eat'? No, you would say to him, 'Prepare something for me to eat. Then get yourself ready and serve me. After I finish eating and drinking, you can eat.' The servant does not get any special thanks for doing what his master commanded. It is the same with you. When you have done everything you are told to do, you should say, 'We are unworthy servants; we have only done the work we should do.'"

Luke 19:11-27 As the people were listening to this, Jesus told them a story because he was near Jerusalem and they thought God's kingdom would appear immediately. He said: "A very important man went to a country far away to be made a king and then to return home. So he called ten of his servants and gave a coin to each servant. He said, 'Do business with this money until I get back.' But the people in the kingdom hated the man. So they sent a group to follow him and say, 'We don't want this man to be our king.'

"But the man became king. When he returned home, he said, 'Call those servants who have my money so I can know how much they earned with it.'

"The first servant came and said, 'Sir, I earned ten coins with the one you gave me.' The king said to the servant, 'Excellent! You are a good servant. Since I can trust you with small things, I will let you rule over ten of my cities.'

"The second servant said, 'Sir, I earned five coins with your one.' The king said to this servant, 'You can rule over five cities.'

"Then another servant came in and said to the king, 'Sir, here is your coin which I wrapped in a piece of cloth and hid. I was afraid of you, because you are a hard man. You even take money that you didn't earn and gather food that you didn't plant.' Then the king said to the servant, 'I will condemn you by your own words, you evil servant. You knew that I am a hard man, taking money that I didn't earn and gathering food that I didn't plant. Why then didn't you put my money in the bank? Then when I came back, my money would have earned some interest.'

"The king said to the men who were standing by, 'Take the coin away from this servant and give it to the servant who earned ten coins.' They said, 'But sir, that servant already has ten coins.' The king said, 'Those who have will be given more, but those who do not have anything will have everything taken away from them. Now where are my enemies who didn't want me to be king? Bring them here and kill them before me.'"

Matthew 25:14-30 Same as above with variations.

(What are you doing with your coin? The coin represents wealth that God has given us—Salvation, The Word, Time, Prayer, etc.)

Matthew 25:34-36 "Then the King will say to the people on his right, 'Come, my Father has given you his blessing. Receive the kingdom God has prepared for you since the world was made. I was hungry, and you gave me food. I was thirsty, and you gave me something to drink. I was alone and away from home, and you invited me into your house. I was without clothes, and you gave me something to wear. I was sick, and you cared for me. I was in prison and you visited me.'

Acts 4:32 The group of believers were united in their hearts and spirit. All those in the group acted as though their private property belonged to everyone in the group. In fact, they shared everything.

Acts 6:1-7 The number of followers was growing. But during this same time, the Greek-speaking followers had an argument with the other Jewish followers. The Greek-speaking widows were not getting their share of the food that was given out every day. The twelve apostles called the whole group of followers together and said, "It is not right for us to stop our work of teaching God's word in order to serve tables. So, brothers and sisters, choose seven of your own men who are good, full of the Spirit and full of wisdom. We will put them in charge of this work. Then we can continue to pray and to teach the word of God."

The whole group liked the idea, so they chose these seven men: Stephen (a man with great faith and full of the Holy Spirit), Philip, Procorus, Nicano, Timon, Parmenas, and Nicolas (a man from Antioch who had become a Jew). Then they put these men before the apostles, who prayed and laid their hands on them.

The word of God was continuing to spread. The group of followers in Jerusalem increased, and a great number of the Jewish priests believed and obeyed.

Romans 12:9-21 Your love must be real. Hate what is evil, and hold on to what is good. Love each other like brothers and sisters. Give each other more honor than you want for yourselves. Don't be lazy but work hard, serving the Lord with all your heart. Be joyful because you have hope. Be patient when trouble comes, and pray at all times. Share with God's people who need help. Bring strangers in need into your homes.

Wish good for those who harm you; wish them well and do not curse them. Be happy with those who are happy, and be sad with those who are sad. Live in peace with each other. Do not be proud, but make friends with those who seem unimportant. Do not think how smart you are.

If someone does wrong to you, do not pay him back by doing wrong to him. Try to do what everyone thinks is right. Do your best to live in peace with everyone. My friends, do not try to punish others when they wrong you, but wait for God to punish them with his anger. It is written: "I will punish those who do wrong; I will repay them," says the Lord. But you should do this;

> "If your enemy is hungry, feed him;
> if he is thirsty, give him a drink.

Doing this will be like pouring burning coals on his head." (Proverbs 25:21-22)

Romans 13: 1-14 All of you must yield to the government rulers. No one rules unless God has given him the power to rule, and no one rules now without that power from God. So those who are against the government are really against what God has commanded. And they will bring punishment on themselves. Those who do right do not have to fear the rulers; only those who do wrong fear them. Do you want to be unafraid of the rulers? Then do what is right, and they will praise you. The ruler is God's servant to help you. But if you do wrong, then be afraid. He has the power to punish; he is God's servant to punish those who do wrong. So you must yield to the government, not only because you might be punished, but because you know it is right.

This is also why you pay taxes. Rulers are working for God and give their time to their work. Pay everyone, then, what you owe. If you owe any kind of tax, pay it. Show respect and honor to them all.

Do not owe people anything, except always owe love to each other, because the person who loves others has obeyed all the law. The law says, "You must not be guilty of adultery. You must not murder anyone. You must not steal. You must not want to take your neighbor's things." All these commands and all others are really only one rule: "Love your neighbor as you love yourself." Love never hurts a neighbor, so loving is obeying all the law.

Do this because we live in an important time. It is now time for you to wake up from your sleep, because our salvation is nearer now than when we first believed. The "night" is almost finished, and the "day" is almost here. So we should stop doing things that belong to darkness and take up the weapons used for fighting in the light. Let us live in a right way, like people who belong to the day. We should not have wild parties or get drunk. There should be no sexual sins of any kind, no fighting or jealousy. But clothe yourselves with the Lord Jesus Christ and forget about satisfying your sinful self.

Romans 14:1-23 (Do not criticize other people and do not cause others to sin) Accept into your group someone who is weak in faith, and do not argue about opinions. One person believes it is right to eat all kinds of food. But another, who is weak, believes it is right to eat only vegetables. The one who knows that it is right to eat any kind of food must not reject the one who eats only vegetables. And the person who eats only vegetables must not think that the one who eats all foods is wrong, because God has accepted that person. You cannot judge another person's servant. The master decides if the servant is doing well or not. And the Lord's servant will do well because the Lord helps him do well.

Some think that one day is more important than another, and others think that every day is the same. Let all be sure in their own mind....

The reason Christ died and rose from the dead to live again was so he would be Lord over both the dead and the living. So why do you judge your brothers or sisters in Christ? And why do you think you are better than they are? ...

For this reason we should stop judging each other. We must make up our minds not to do anything that will make another Christian sin....

So let us try to do what makes peace and helps one another....

Your beliefs about these things should be kept secret between you and God. People are happy if they can do what they think is right without feeling guilty. But those who eat something without being sure it is right are wrong because they did not believe it was right. Anything that is done without believing it is right is a sin.

Romans 15:1-10 We who are strong in faith should help the weak with their weaknesses, and not please only ourselves. Let each of us please our neighbors for their good, to help them be stronger in faith. Even Christ did not live to please himself....

1 Corinthians 4:9-13 But it seems to me that God has put us apostles in last place, like those sentenced to die. We are like a show for the whole world to see—angles and people. We are fools for Christ's sake, but you are very wise in Christ. We are weak, but you are strong. You receive honor, but we are shamed. Even to this very hour we do not have enough to eat or drink or to wear. We are often beaten, and we have no homes in which to live. We work hard with our own hands for our food. When people curse us, we bless them. When they hurt us, we put up with it. When they tell evil lies about us, we speak nice words about them. Even today, we are treated as though we were the garbage of the world—the filth of the earth.

2 Corinthians 6:6-7 We show we are servants of God by our pure lives, our understanding, patience, and kindness, by the Holy Spirit, by true love, by speaking the truth, and by God's power. We use our right living to defend ourselves against everything.

2 Corinthians 8:14-15 At this time you have plenty. What you have can help others who are in need. Then later, when they have plenty, they can help you when you are in need, and all will be equal. As it is written in the Scriptures, "The person who gathered more did not have to much, nor did the person who gathered less have too little."

2 Corinthians 9:6-9 Remember this: The person who plants a little will have a small harvest, but the person who plants a lot will have a big harvest. Each one should give as you have decided in your heart to give. You should not be sad when you give, and you should not give because you feel forced to give. God loves the person who gives happily. And God can give you more blessings than you need. Then you will always have plenty of everything—enough to give to every good work. It is written in the Scriptures:

> "He gives freely to the poor.
> The things he does are right and will continue forever." (Psalm 112:9)

Ephesians 4:2-13 Always be humble, gently, and patient, accepting each other in love. You are joined together with peace through the Spirit, so make every effort to continue together in this way. There is one body and one Spirit, and God called you to have one hope. There is one Lord, one faith, and one baptism. There is one God and Father of everything. He rules everything and is everywhere and is in everything.

Christ gave each one of us the special gift of grace, showing how generous he is....

Ephesians 4:25-32 So you must stop telling lies. Tell each other the truth, because we all belong to each other in the same body. When you are angry, do not sin, and be sure to stop being angry before the end of the day. Do not give the devil a way to defeat you. Those who are stealing must stop stealing and start working. They should earn an honest living for themselves. Then they will have something to share with those who are poor.

When you talk, do not say harmful things, but say what people need—words that will help others become stronger. Then what you say will do good to those who listen to you. And do not make the Holy Spirit sad. The Spirit is God's proof that you belong to him. God gave you the Spirit to show that God will make you free when the final day comes. Do not be bitter or angry or mad. Never shout angrily or say things to hurt others. Never do anything evil. Be kind and loving to each other, and forgive each other just as God forgave you in Christ.

Ephesians 5:1-5 You are God's children whom he loves, so try to be like him. Live a life of love just as Christ loved us and gave himself for us as a sweet-smelling offering and sacrifice to God.

But there must be no sexual sin among you, or any king of evil or greed. Those things are not right for God's holy people. Also, there must be no evil talk among you, and you must not speak foolishly or tell evil jokes. These things are not right for you. Instead, you should be giving thanks to God. You can be sure of this: No one will have a place in the kingdom of Christ and of God who sins sexually, or does evil things, or is greedy. Anyone who is greedy is serving a false god.

Philippians 2:3-11 When you do things, do not let selfishness or pride be your guide. Instead, be humble and give more honor to others than to yourselves. Do not be interested only in your own life, but be interested in the lives of others.

> In your lives you must think and act like Christ Jesus.
> Christ himself was like God in everything.
> > But he did not think that being equal with God was something to be used for his own benefit.
> But he gave up his place with God and made himself nothing.
> > He was born to be a man
> > and become like a servant.
> And when he was living as a man,
> > he humbled himself and was fully obedient to God,
> > even when that caused his death—death on a cross.
> So God raised him to the highest place.
> > God made his name greater than every other name
> so that every knee will bow to the name of Jesus—
> > everyone in heaven, on earth, and under the earth.
> And everyone will confess that Jesus Christ is Lord
> > and bring glory to God the Father.

Philippians 4:5 Let everyone see that you are gentle and kind. The Lord is coming soon.

Colossians 3:5-17 So put all evil things out of your life: sexual sinning, doing evil, letting evil thoughts control you, wanting things that are evil, and greed. This is really serving a false god. These things make God angry. In your past, evil life you also did these things.

But now also put these things out of your life: anger, bad temper, doing or saying things to hurt others, and using evil words when you talk. Do not lie to each other. You have left your old sinful life and the things you did before. You have begun to live the new life, in which you are being made new and are becoming like the One who made you. This new life brings you the true knowledge of God. In the new life there is no difference between Greeks and Jews, those who are circumcised and those who are not circumcised, or people who are foreigners, or Scythians. There is no difference between slaves and free people. But Christ is in all believers, and Christ is all that is important.

God has chosen you and made you his holy people. He loves you. So always do these things: Show mercy to others, be kind, humble, gentle, and patient. Get along with each other, and forgive each other. If someone does wrong to you, forgive that person because the Lord forgave you. Do all these things: but most important, love each other. Love is what holds you all together in perfect unity. Let the peace that Christ gives control your thinking, because you were all called together in one body to have peace. Always be thankful. Let the teaching of Christ live in you richly. Use all wisdom to teach and instruct each other by singing psalms, hymns, and spiritual songs with thankfulness in your hearts to God. Everything you do or say should be done to obey Jesus your Lord. And in all you do, give thanks to God the Father through Jesus.

1 Timothy 5:1-25 (Rules for living with others) Do not speak angrily to an older man, but plead with him as if he were your father. Treat younger men like brothers, older women like mothers, and younger women like sisters. Always treat them in a pure way.

Take care of widows who are truly widows. But if a widow has children or grandchildren, let them first learn to do their duty to their own family and to repay their parents or grandparents. That pleases God. The true widow, who is all alone, puts her hope in God and continues to pray night and day for God's help. But the widow who uses her life to please herself is really dead while she is alive. Tell the believers to do these things so that no one can criticize them. Whoever does not care for his own relatives, especially his own family members, has turned against the faith and is worse than someone who does not believe in God.

To be on the list of widows, a woman must be at least sixty years old. She must have been faithful to her husband. She must be know for her good works—works such as raising her children, welcoming strangers, washing the feet of God's people, helping those in trouble, and giving her life to do all kinds of good deeds.

But do not put younger widows on that list....So I want the younger widows to marry, have children, and manage their homes. Then no enemy will have any reason to criticize them. But some have already turned away to follow Satan.

If any woman who is a believer has widows in her family, she should care for them herself. The church should not have to care for them. Then it will be able to take care of those who are truly widows.

The elders who lead the church well should receive double honor, especially those who work hard by speaking and teaching, because the Scripture says: "When an ox is working in the grain, do not cover its mouth to keep it from eating," and "A worker should be given his pay."

Do not listen to someone who accuses an elder, without two or three witnesses. Tell those who continue sinning that they are wrong. Do this in front of the whole church so that the others will have a warning.

Before God and Christ Jesus and the chosen angels, I command you to do these things without showing favor of any kind to anyone.

Think carefully before you lay your hands on anyone, and don't share in the sins of others. Keep yourself pure.

Stop drinking only water, but drink a little wine to help your stomach and your frequent sicknesses.

The sins of some people are easy to see even before they are judged, but the sins of others are seen only later. So also good deeds are easy to see, but even those that are not easily seen cannot stay hidden.

1 Timothy 6:11-12 But you, man of God, run away from all those things. Instead, live in the right way, serve God, have faith, love, patience, and gentleness. Fight the good fight of faith, grabbing hold of the life that continues forever. You were called to have that life when you confessed the good confession before many witnesses.

2 Timothy 2:14-26 (A worker pleasing to God) Continue teaching these things, warning people in God's presence not to argue about words. It does not help anyone, and it ruins those who listen. Make every effort to give yourself to God as the kind of person he will accept. Be a worker who is not ashamed and who uses the true teaching in the right way. Stay away from foolish, useless talk, because that will lead people further away from God. Their evil teaching will spread like a sickness inside the body. Hymenaeus and Philetus are like that. They have left the true teaching, saying that the rising from the dead has already taken place, and so they are destroying the faith of some people. But God's strong foundation continues to stand. These words are written on the seal: "The Lord knows those who belong to him," and "Everyone who wants to belong to the Lord must stop doing wrong."

In a large house there are not only things made of gold and silver, but also things made of wood and clay. Some things are used for special purposes, and others are made for ordinary jobs. All who make themselves clean from evil will be used for special purposes. They will be made holy, useful to the Master, ready to do any good work.

But run away from the evil young people like to do. Try hard to live right and to have faith, love, and peace, together with those who trust in the Lord from pure hearts. Stay away from foolish and stupid arguments, because you know they grow into quarrels. And a servant of the Lord must not quarrel but must be kind to everyone, a good teacher, and patient. The Lord's servant must gently teach those who disagree. Then maybe God will let them change their minds so they can accept the truth. And they may wake up and escape from the trap of the devil, who catches them to do what he wants.

Hebrews 13:1-9 Keep on loving each other as brothers and sisters. Remember to welcome strangers, because some who have done this have welcomed angels without knowing it. Remember those who are in prison as if you were in prison with them. Remember those who are suffering as if you were suffering with them.

Marriage should be honored by everyone, and husband and wife should keep their marriage pure. God will judge as guilty those who take part in sexual sins. Keep you lives free from the love of money, and be satisfied with what you have. God has said,

> "I will never leave you;
> I will never forget you." (Deuteronomy 31:6)
> So we can be sure when we say,
> "I will not be afraid, because the Lord is my helper.
> People can't do anything to me." (Psalm 118:6)

Remember your leaders who taught God's message to you. Remember how they lived and died, and copy their faith. Jesus Christ is the same yesterday, today, and forever.

Do not let all kinds of strange teachings lead you into the wrong way. Your hearts should be strengthened by God's grace, not by obeying rules about foods, which do not help those who obey them.

James 2:1-13 My dear brothers and sisters, as believers in our glorious Lord Jesus Christ, never think some people are more important than others. Suppose someone comes into your church meeting wearing nice clothes and a gold ring. At the same time a poor person comes in wearing old, dirty clothes. You show special attention to the one wearing nice clothes and say, "Please, sit here in this good seat." But you say to the poor person, "Stand over there," or, "Sit on the floor by my feet." What are you doing? You are making some people more important than others, and with evil thoughts you are deciding that one person is better.

Listen, my dear brothers and sisters! God chose the poor in the world to be rich with faith and to receive the kingdom God promised to those who love him. But you show no respect to the poor. The rich are always trying to control your lives. They are the ones who take you to court. And they are the ones who speak against Jesus, who owns you.

This royal law is found in the Scriptures: "Love your neighbor as you love yourself." If you obey this law, you are doing right. But if you treat one person as being more important than another, you are sinning. You are guilty of breaking God's law. A person who follows all of God's law but fails to obey even one command is guilty of breaking all the commands in that law. The same God who said, "You must not be guilty of adultery," also said, "you must not murder anyone." So if you do not take part in adultery but you murder someone, you are guilty of breaking all of God's law. In everything you say and do, remember that you will be judged by the law that makes people free. So you must show mercy to others, or God will not show mercy to you when he judges you. But the person who shows mercy can stand without fear at the judgment.

James 5:13-18 Anyone who is having troubles should pray. Anyone who is happy should sing praises. Anyone who is sick should call the church's elders. They should pray for and pour oil on the person in the name of the Lord. And the prayer that is said with faith will make the sick person well; the Lord will heal that person. And if the person has sinned, the sins will be forgiven. Confess your sins to each other and pray for each other so God can heal you. When a believing person prays, great things happen. Elijah was a human being just like us. He prayed that it would not rain, and it did not rain on the land for three and half years! Then Elijah prayed again, and the rain came down from the sky, and the land produced crops again.

1 Peter 2:23 People insulted Christ, but he did not insult them in return. Christ suffered, but he did not threaten. He let God, the One who judges rightly, take care of him.

1 Peter 3:8-18 Finally, all of you should be in agreement, understanding each other, loving each other as family, being kind and humble. Do not do wrong to repay a wrong, and do not insult to repay an insult. But repay with a blessing, because you yourselves were called to do this so that you might receive a blessing. The Scripture says,

> "A person must do these things
> to enjoy life and have many happy days.

He must not say evil things,
   and he must not tell lies.
He must stop doing evil and do good.
   He must look for peace and work for it.
The Lord sees the good people
   and listens to their prayers.
But the Lord is against
   those who do evil." (Psalm 34:12-16)
If you are trying hard to do good, no one can really hurt you.
But even if you suffer for doing right, you are blessed.
"Don't be afraid of what they fear;
do not dread those things." (Isaiah 8:12-13)

But respect Christ as the holy Lord in your hearts. Always be ready to answer everyone who asks you to explain about the hope you have, but answer in a gentle way and with respect. Keep a clear conscience so that those who speak evil of your good life in Christ will be made ashamed. It is better to suffer for doing good than for doing wrong if that is what God wants. Christ himself suffered for sins once. He was not guilty, but he suffered for those who are guilty to bring you to God. His body was killed, but he was made alive in the spirit.

2 Peter 1:5-8 Because you have these blessings, do your best to add these things to your lives: to your faith, add goodness; and to your goodness, add knowledge; and to your knowledge, add self-control; and to your self-control, add patience; and to your patience, add service for God; and to your service for God, add kindness for your brothers and sisters in Christ; and to this kindness, add love. If all these things are in you and are growing, they will help you to be useful and productive in your knowledge of our Lord Jesus Christ.

1 John 3:17-18 Suppose someone has enough to live and sees a brother or sister in need, but does not help. Then God's love is not living in that person. My children, we should love people not only with words and talk, but by our actions and true caring.

Titus 3:1-11 Remind the believers to yield to the authority of rulers and government leaders, to obey them, to be ready to do good, to speak no evil about anyone, to live in peace, and to be gentle and polite to all people.

In the past we also were foolish. We did not obey, we were wrong, and we were slaves to many things our bodies wanted and enjoyed. We spent our lives doing evil and being jealous. People hated us, and we hated each other. But when the kindness and love of God our Savior was shown, he saved us because of his mercy. It was not because of good deeds we did to be right with him. He saved us through the washing that made us new people through the Holy Spirit. God poured out richly upon us that Holy Spirit through Jesus Christ our Savior. Being made right with God by his grace, we could have the hope of receiving the life that never ends.

This teaching is true, and I want you to be sure the people understand these things. Then those who believe in God will be careful to use their lives for doing good. These things are good and will help everyone.

But stay away from those who have foolish arguments and talk about useless family histories and argue and quarrel about the law. Those things are worth nothing and will not help anyone. After a first and second warning, avoid someone who causes arguments. You can know that such people are evil and sinful; their own sins prove them wrong.

Titus 3:14 Our people must learn to use their lives for doing good deeds to provide what is necessary so that their lives will not be useless.

God Wants All To Be Saved

Matthew 18:10-14 "Be careful. Don't think these little children are worth nothing. I tell you that they have angels in heaven who are always with my Father in heaven.

"If a man has a hundred sheep but one of the sheep gets lost, he will leave the other ninety-nine on the hill and go to look for the lost sheep. I tell you the truth, he is happier about that one sheep than about the ninety-nine that were never lost. In the same way, your Father in heaven does not want any of these little children to be lost."

Acts 10:34-36 Peter began to speak: "I really understand now that to God every person is the same. In every country God accepts anyone who worships him and does what is right. You know the message that God has sent to the people of Israel is the Good News that peace has come through Jesus Christ. Jesus is the Lord of all people!"

1 Timothy 2:3 This is good, and it pleases God our Savior, who wants all people to be saved and to know the truth.

2 Peter 3:8-9 But do not forget this one thing, dear friends: To the Lord one day is as a thousand years, and a thousand years is as one day. The Lord is not slow in doing what he promised—the way some people understand slowness. But God is being patient with you. He does not want anyone to be lost, but he wants all people to change their hearts and lives.

Romans 3:26 And God gave Jesus to show today that he does what is right. God did this so he could judge rightly and so he could make right any person who has faith in Jesus.

Hebrews 2:10 God is the One who made all things, and all things are for his glory. He wanted to have many children share his glory, so he made the One who leads people to salvation perfect through suffering.

Story About Workers

Matthew 20:1-16 "The kingdom of heaven is like a person who owned some land. One morning, he went out very early to hire some people to work in his vineyard. The man agreed to pay the workers one coin for working that day. Then he sent them into the vineyard to work. About nine o'clock the man went to the marketplace and saw some other people standing there, doing nothing. So he said to them, 'If you go and work in my vineyard, I will pay you what your work is worth.' So they went to work in the vineyard. The man went out again about twelve o'clock and three o'clock and did the same thing. About five o'clock the man went to the marketplace again and saw others standing there. He asked them, 'Why did you stand here all day doing nothing?' They answered, 'No one gave us a job.' The man said to them, 'Then you can go and work in my vineyard.'

"At the end of the day, the owner of the vineyard said to the boss of all the workers, 'Call the workers and pay them. Start with the last people I hired and end with those I hired first.'

"When the workers who were hired at five o'clock came to get their pay, each received one coin. When the workers who were hired first came to get their pay, they thought they would be paid more than the others. But each one of them also received one coin. When they got their coin, they complained to the man who owned the land. They said, 'Those people were hired last and worked only one hour. But you paid them the same as you paid us who worked hard all day in the hot sun.' But the man who owned the vineyard said to one of those workers, 'Friend, I am being fair to you. You agreed to work for one coin. So take your pay and go. I want to give the man who was hired last the same pay that I gave you. I can do what I want with my own money. Are you jealous because I am good to those people?'

"So those who have the last place now will have the first place in the future, and those who have the first place now will have the last place in the future."

A Jewish Rabbi on television said, "How can a person who is good his entire life go to hell just because he doesn't accept Jesus as his Savior, and a person who is bad his entire life go to heaven if he accepts Jesus as his Savior at the end of his life ..." Jealousy.

Those Who Reject Jesus

Matthew 22:1-14 Jesus again used stories to teach the people. He said, "The kingdom of heaven is like a king who prepared a wedding feast for his son. The king invited some people to the feast. When the feast was ready, the king sent his servants to tell the people, but they refused to come.

"Then the king sent other servants, saying, 'Tell those who have been invited that my feast is ready. I have killed my best bulls and calves for the dinner, and everything is ready. Come to the wedding feast.'

"But the people refused to listen to the servants and left to do other things. One went to work in his field, and another went to his business. Some of the other people grabbed the servants, beat them, and killed them. The king was furious and sent his army to kill the murderers and burn the city.

"After that, the king said to his servants, 'The wedding feast is ready. I invited those people, but they were not worthy to come. So go to the street corners and invite everyone you find to come to my feast.' So the servants went into the streets and gathered all the people they could find, both good and bad. And the wedding hall was filled with guests.

"When the king came in to see the guests, he saw a man who was not dressed for a wedding. The king said, 'Friend, how were you allowed to come in here? You are not dressed for a wedding.' But the man said nothing. So the king told some servants, 'Tie this man's hands and feet. Throw him out into the darkness, where people will cry and grind their teeth with pain.'

"Yes, many people are invited, but only a few are chosen."

Luke 14:15-24 Same as above with variations.

Matthew 21:28-32 "Tell me what you think about this: A man had two sons. He went to the first son and said, 'Son, go and work today in my vineyard.' The son answered, 'I will not go.' But later the son changed his mind and went. Then the father went to the other son and said, 'Son, go and work today in my vineyard.' The son answered, 'Yes, sir, I will go and work,' but he did not go. Which of the two sons obeyed his father?"

The priests and leaders answered, "The first son."

Jesus said to them, "I tell you the truth, the tax collectors and the prostitutes will enter the kingdom of God before you do. John came to show you the right way to live. You did not believe him, but the tax collectors and prostitutes believed him. Even after seeing this, you still refused to change your ways and believe him."

Mark 12:1-12 (A story about God's Son.) Jesus began to use stories to teach the people. He said, "A man planted a vineyard. He put a wall around it and dug a hole for a winepress and built a tower. Then he leased the land to some farmers and left for a trip. When it was time for the grapes to be picked, he sent a servant to the farmers to get his share of the grapes. But the farmers grabbed the servant and beat him and sent him away empty-handed. Then the man sent another servant. They hit him on the head and showed no respect for him. So the man sent another servant, whom they killed. The man sent many other servants; the farmers beat some of them and killed others.

"The man had one person left to send, his son whom he loved. He sent him last of all, saying, 'They will respect my son.'

But the farmers said to each other, 'This son will inherit the vineyard. If we kill him, it will be ours.' So they took the son, killed him, and threw him out of the vineyard.

"So what will the owner of the vineyard do? He will come and kill those farmers and will give the vineyard to other farmers. Surely you have read this Scripture:

> 'The stone that the builders rejected
> became the cornerstone.
> The Lord did this,
> and it is wonderful to us.'" (Psalm 118:22-23)

The Jewish leaders knew that the story was about them. So they wanted to find a way to arrest Jesus, but they were afraid of the people. So the leaders left him and went away.

Matthew 21:33-46 Same as above with variations.
Luke 20:9-19 Same as above with variations.

Power Of —Faith In Christ — Makes Us Right, Not The Law

Romans 8:24-25 We were saved, and we have this hope. If we see what we are waiting for, that is not really hope. People do not hope for something they already have. But we are hoping for something we do not have yet, and we are waiting for it patiently.

Matthew 21:18-22 Early the next morning, as Jesus was going back to the city, he became hungry. Seeing a fig tree beside the road, Jesus went to it, but there were no figs on the tree, only leaves. So Jesus said to the tree, "You will never again have fruit." The tree immediately dried up.

When his followers saw this, they were amazed. They asked, "How did the fig tree dry up so quickly?"

Jesus answered, "I tell you the truth, if you have faith and do not doubt, you will be able to do what I did to this tree and even more. You will be able to say to this mountain, 'Go, fall into the sea.' And if you have faith, it will happen. If you believe, you will get anything you ask for in prayer."

Mark 11:22-25 Same as above with variations.

Luke 17:5-6 The apostles said to the Lord, "Give us more faith!"

The Lord said, "If your faith were the size of a mustard seed, you could say to this mulberry tree, 'Dig yourself up and plant yourself in the sea,' and it would obey you.

Luke 18:1-8 Then Jesus used this story to teach his followers that they should always pray and never lose hope. "In a certain town there was a judge who did not respect God or care about people. In that same town there was a widow who kept coming to this judge, saying, 'Give me my rights against my enemy.' For a while the judge refused to help her. But afterwards, he thought to himself, 'Even though I don't respect God or care about people, I will see that she gets her rights. Otherwise she will continue to bother me until I am worn out.'"

The Lord said, "Listen to what the unfair judge said. God will always give what is right to his people who cry to him night and day, and he will not be slow to answer them. I tell you, God will help his people quickly. But when the Son of Man comes again, will he find those on earth who believe in him?"

2 Corinthians 4:18 We set our eyes not on what we see but on what we cannot see. What we see will last only a short time, but what we cannot see will last forever.

Acts 3:16 "It was faith in Jesus that made this crippled man well. You can see this man, and you know him. He was made completely well because of trust in Jesus, and you all saw it happen!"

Romans 3:19-31 We know that the law's commands are for those who have the law. This stops all excuses and brings the whole world under God's judgment, because no one can be made right with God by following the law. The law only shows us our sin.

But God has a way to make people right with him without the law, and he has now shown us that way which the law and the prophets told us about. God makes people right with himself through their faith in Jesus Christ. This is true for all who believe in Christ, because all people are the same: All have sinned and are not good enough for God's glory, and all need to be made right with God by his grace, which is a free gift. They need to be made free from sin through Jesus Christ. God gave him as a way to forgive sin through faith in the blood of Jesus' death. This showed that God always does what is right and fair, as in the past when he was patient and did not punish people for their sins. And God gave Jesus to show today that he does what is right. God did this so he could judge rightly and so he could make right any person who has faith in Jesus.

So do we have a reason to brag about ourselves? No! And why not? It is the way of faith that stops all bragging, not the way of trying to obey the law. A person is made right with God through faith, not through obeying the law. Is God only the God of the Jews? Is he not also the God of those who are not Jews? Of course he is, because there is only one God. He will make Jews right with him by their faith, and he will also make those who are not Jews right with him through their faith. So do we destroy the law by following the way of faith? No! **Faith causes us to be what the law truly wants**.

Romans 4:9-12 Is this blessing only for those who are circumcised or also for those who are not circumcised? We have already said that God accepted Abraham's faith and that faith made him right with God. So how did this happen? Did God accept Abraham before or after he was circumcised? It was before his circumcision. Abraham was circumcised to show that he was right with God through faith before he was circumcised. So Abraham is the father of all those who believe but are not circumcised; he is the father of all believers who are accepted as being right with God. And Abraham is also the father of those who have been circumcised and who live following the faith that our father Abraham had before he was circumcised.

Romans 4:13-25 Abraham and his descendants received the promise that they would get the whole world. He did not receive that promise through the law, but through being right with God by his faith. If people could receive what

God promised by following the law, then faith is worthless. And God's promise to Abraham is worthless, because the law can only bring God's anger. But if there is no law, there is nothing to disobey.

So people receive God's promise by having faith. This happens so the promise can be a free gift. Then all of Abraham's children can have that promise. It is not only for those who live under the law of Moses but for anyone who lives with faith like that of Abraham, who is the father of us all. As it is written in the Scriptures: "I am making you a father of many nations." This is true before God, the God Abraham believed, the God who gives life to the dead and who creates something out of nothing.

There was no hope that Abraham would have children. But Abraham believed God and continued hoping, and so he became the father of many nations. As God told him, "Your descendants also will be too many to count." Abraham was almost a hundred years old, much past the age for having children, and Sarah could not have children. Abraham thought about all this, but his faith in God did not become weak. He never doubted that God would keep his promise, and he never stopped believing. He grew stronger in his faith and gave praise to God. Abraham felt sure that God was able to do what he had promised. So, "God accepted Abraham's faith, and that faith made him right with God." Those words ("God accepted Abraham's faith") were written not only for Abraham but also for us. God will accept us also because we believe in the One who raised Jesus our Lord from the dead. Jesus was given to die for our sins, and he was raised from the dead to make us right with God.

Romans 5:1-11 Since we have been made right with God by our faith, we have peace with God. This happened through our Lord Jesus Christ, who has brought us into that blessing of God's grace that we now enjoy. And we are happy because of the hope we have of sharing God's glory. We also have joy with our troubles, because we know that these troubles produce patience. And patience produces character, and character produces hope. And this hope will never disappoint us, because God has poured out his love to fill our hearts. He gave us his love through the Holy Spirit, whom God has given to us.

When we were unable to help ourselves, at the moment of our need, Christ died for us, although we were living against God. Very few people will die to save the life of someone else. Although perhaps for a good person someone might possible die. But God shows his great love for us in this way: Christ died for us while we were still sinners.

So through Christ we will surely be saved from God's anger, because we have been made right with God by the blood of Christ's death. While we were God's enemies, he made friends with us through the death of his Son. Surely, now that we are his friends, he will save us through his Son's life. And not only that, but now we are also very happy in God through our Lord Jesus Christ. Through him we are now God's friends again.

Romans 9:30-33 So what does all this mean? Those who are not Jews were not trying to make themselves right with God, but they were made right with God because of their faith. The people of Israel tried to follow a law to make themselves right with God. But they did not succeed, because they tried to make themselves right by the things they did instead of trusting in God to make them right. They stumbled over the stone that causes people to stumble. As it is written in the Scripture:

> "I will put in Jerusalem a stone that causes people
> to stumble,
> a rock that makes them fall.
> Anyone who trusts in him will never be
> disappointed." (Isaiah 8:14; 28:16)

Romans 10:4-13 Christ ended the law so that everyone who believes in him may be right with God.

Moses writes about being made right by following the law. He says, "A person who obeys these things will live because of them." But this is what the Scripture says about being made right through faith: "Don't say to yourself, 'Who will go up into heaven?'" (That means, "Who will go up to heaven and bring Christ down to earth?") "And do not say, 'Who will go down into the world below?'" (That means, "Who will go down and bring Christ up from the dead?") This is what the Scripture says: "The word is near you; it is in your mouth and in your heart." That is the teaching of faith that we are telling. If you use your mouth to say, "Jesus is Lord," and if you believe in your heart that God raised Jesus from the dead, you will be saved. We believe with our hearts, and so we are made right with God. And we use our mouths to say that we believe, and so we are saved. As the Scripture says, "Anyone who trusts in him will never be disappointed." That Scripture says "anyone" because there is no difference between those who are Jews and those who are not. The same Lord is the Lord of all and gives many blessings to all who trust in him, as the Scripture says, "Anyone who calls on the Lord will be saved."

Ephesians 3:12 In Christ we can come before God with freedom and without fear. We can do this through faith in Christ.

Philippians 2:17 Your faith makes you offer your lives as a sacrifice in serving God. If I have to offer my own blood with your sacrifice, I will be happy and full of joy with all of you.

Philippians 3:8-9 Not only those things, but I think that all things are worth nothing compared with the greatness of knowing Christ Jesus my Lord. Because of him, I have lost all those things, and now I know they are worthless trash. This allows me to have Christ and to belong to him. Now I am right with God, not because I followed the law, but because I believed in Christ. God uses my faith to make me right with him.

Colossians 2:12 When you were baptized, you were buried with Christ, and you were raised up with him through your faith in God's power that was shown when he raised Christ from the dead.

2 Thessalonians 1:11 That is why we always pray for you, asking our God to help you live the kind of life he called you to live. We pray that with his power God will help you do the good things you want and perform the works that come from your faith.

2 Thessalonians 2:13 Brothers and sisters, whom the Lord loves, God chose you from the beginning to be saved. So we must always thank God for you. You are saved by the Spirit that makes you holy and by your faith in the truth.

1 Timothy 6:11-12 But you, man of God, run away from all those things. Instead, live in the right way, serve God, have faith, love, patience, and gentleness. Fight the good fight of faith, grabbing hold of the life that continues forever. You were called to have that life when you confessed the good confession before many witnesses.

Hebrews 10:22 Let us come near to God with a sincere heart and a sure faith, because we have been made free from a guilty conscience, and our bodies have been washed with pure water.

Hebrews 11:1-40 Faith means being sure of the things we hope for and knowing that something is real even if we do not see it. Faith is the reason we remember great people who lived in the past.

It is by faith we understand that the whole world was made by God's command so what we see was made by something that cannot be seen.

It was by faith that Abel offered God a better sacrifice than Cain did. God said he was pleased with the gifts Abel offered and called Abel a good man because of his faith. Abel died, but through his faith he is still speaking.

It was by faith that Enoch was taken to heaven so he would not die. He could not be found, because God had taken him away. Before he was taken, the Scripture says that he was a man who truly pleased God. Without faith no one can please God. Anyone who comes to God must believe that he is real and that he rewards those who truly want to find him.

It was by faith that Noah heard God's warning about things he could not yet see. He obeyed God and built a large boat to save his family. By his faith, Noah showed that the world was wrong, and he became one of those who are made right with God through faith.

It was by faith Abraham obeyed God's call to go to another place God promised to give him....

All these great people died in faith. They did not get the things that God promised his people, but they saw them coming far in the future and were glad....

It was by faith that Abraham, when God tested him, offered his son Isaac as a sacrifice....

It was by faith that Isaac blessed the future of Jacob and Esau. It was by faith that Jacob, as he was dying, blessed each one of Joseph's sons. Then he worshiped as he leaned on the top of his walking stick.

It was by faith that Joseph, while he was dying, spoke about the Israelites leaving Egypt and gave instructions about what to do with his body.

It was by faith that Moses' parents hid him for three months after he was born....

It was by faith that Moses, when he grew up, refused to be called the son of the king of Egypt's daughter....It was by faith that Moses prepared the Passover and spread the blood on the doors so the one who brings death would not kill the firstborn sons of Israel.

It was by faith that the people crossed the Red Sea as if it were dry land....

It was by faith that the walls of Jericho fell after the people had marched around them for seven days.

It was by faith that Rahab, the prostitute, welcomed the spies and was not killed with those who refused to obey God.

Do I need to give more examples? I do not have time to tell you about Gideon, Barak, Samson, Jephthah, David, Samuel, and the prophets. Through their faith they defeated kingdoms. They did what was right, received God's promises, and shut the mouths of lions....

All these people are known for their faith, but none of them received what God had promised. God planned to give us something better so that they would be made perfect, but only together with us.

Hebrews 12:1-3 We have around us many people whose lives tell us what faith means. So let us run the race that is before us and never give up. We should remove from our lives anything that would get in the way and the sin that so easily holds us back. Let us look only to Jesus, the One who began our faith and who makes it perfect. He suffered death on the cross. But he accepted the shame as if it were nothing because of the joy that God put before him. And now he is sitting at the right side of God's throne. Think about Jesus' example. He held on while wicked people were doing evil things to him. So do not get tired and stop trying.

James 1:2-3 My brothers and sisters, when you have many kinds of troubles, you should be full of joy, because you know that these troubles test your faith, and this will give you patience.

1 John 5:3-4 Loving God means obeying his commands. And God's commands are not too hard for us, because everyone who is a child of God conquers the world. And this is the victory that conquers the world—our faith.

James 2:14-26 My brothers and sisters, if people say they have faith, but do nothing, their faith is worth nothing. Can faith like that save them? A brother or sister in Christ might need clothes or food. If you say to that person, "God be with you! I hope you stay warm and get plenty to eat," but you do not give what that person needs, your words are worth nothing. In the same way, faith that is alone—that does nothing—is dead.

Someone might say, "You have faith, but I have deeds." Show me your faith without doing anything, and I will show you my faith by what I do. You believe there is one God. Good! But the demons believe that, too, and they tremble with fear.

You foolish person! Must you be shown that faith that does nothing is worth nothing? Abraham, our ancestor, was made right with God by what he did when he offered his son Isaac on the altar. So you see that Abraham's faith and the things he did worked together. His faith was made perfect by what he did. This shows the full meaning of the Scripture that says: "Abraham believed God, and God accepted Abraham's faith, and that faith made him right with God." And Abraham was called God's friend. So you see that people are made right with God by what they do, not by faith only.

Another example is Rahab, a prostitute, who was made right with God by something she did. She welcomed the spies into her home and helped them escape by a different road.

Just as a person's body that does not have a spirit is dead, so faith that does nothing is dead!

1 Peter 1:5-9 God's power protects you through your faith until salvation is shown to you at the end of time. This make you very happy, even though now for a short time different kinds of troubles may make you sad. These troubles come to prove that your faith is pure. This purity of faith is worth more than gold, which can be proved to be pure by fire but will ruin. But the purity of your faith will bring you praise and glory and honor when Jesus Christ is shown to you. You have not seen Christ, but still you love him. You cannot see him now, but you believe in him. So you are filled with joy that cannot be explained, a joy full of glory. And you are receiving the goal of your faith—the salvation of your souls.

1 Peter 1:21 Through Christ you believe in God, who raised Christ from the dead and gave him glory. So your faith and your hope are in God.

2 Peter 1:5-8 Because you have these blessings, do your best to add these things to your lives: to your faith, add goodness; and to your goodness, add knowledge; and to your knowledge, add self-control; and to your self-control, add patience; and to your patience, add service for God; and to your service for God, add kindness for your brothers and sisters in Christ; and to this kindness, add love. If all these things are in you and are growing, they will help you to be useful and productive in your knowledge of our Lord Jesus Christ.

Galatians 2:15-21 We were not born as non-Jewish "sinners," but as Jews. Yet we know that a person is made right with God not by following the law, but by trusting in Jesus Christ. So we, too, have put our faith in Christ Jesus, that we might be made right with God because we trusted in Christ. It is not because we followed the law, because no one can be made right with God by following the law.

We Jews came to Christ, trying to be made right with God, and it became clear that we are sinners, too. Does this mean that Christ encourages sin? No! But I would really be wrong to begin teaching again those things that I gave up. It was the law that put me to death, and I died to the law so that I can now live for God. I was put to death on the cross with Christ, and I do not live anymore—it is Christ who lives in me. I still live in my body, but I live by faith in the Son of God who loved me and gave himself to save me. By saying these things I am not going against God's grace. Just the opposite, if the law could make us right with God, then Christ's death would be useless.

Galatians 3:1-29 (Blessing Comes Through Faith) You people in Galatia were told very clearly about the death of Jesus Christ on the cross. But you were foolish; you let someone trick you. Tell me this one thing: How did you receive the Holy Spirit? Did you receive the Spirit by following the law? No, you received the Spirit because you heard the Good News and believed it. You began your life in Christ by the Spirit. Now are you trying to make it complete by your own power? That is foolish. Were all your experiences wasted? I hope not! Does God give you the Spirit and work miracles among you because you follow the law? No, he does these things because you heard the Good News and believed it.

The Scriptures say the same thing about Abraham: "Abraham believed God, and God accepted Abraham's faith, and that faith made him right with God." So you should know that the true children of Abraham are those who have faith. The Scriptures, telling what would happen in the future, said that God would make the non-Jewish people right through their faith. This Good News was told to Abraham beforehand, as the Scripture says: "All nations will be blessed through you." So all who believe as Abraham believed are blessed just as Abraham was. But those who depend on following the law to make them right are under a curse, because the Scriptures say, "Anyone will be cursed who does not always obey what is written in the Book of the Law." Now it is clear that no one can be made right with God by the law, because the Scriptures say, "Those who are right with God will live by trusting in him." **The law is not based on faith**. It says, "A person who obeys these things will live because of them." Christ took away the curse the law put on us. He changed places with us and put himself under that curse. It is written in the Scriptures, "Anyone whose body is displayed on a tree is cursed." Christ did this so that God's blessing promised to Abraham might come through Jesus Christ to those who are not Jews. Jesus died so that by our believing we could receive the Spirit that God promised.

Brothers and sisters, let us think in human terms: Even an agreement made between two persons is firm. After that agreement is accepted by both people, no one can stop it or add anything to it. God made promises both to Abraham and to his descendant. God did not say, "and to your descendants." That would mean many people. But God said, "and to your descendant." That means only one person; that person is Christ. This is what I mean: God had an agreement with Abraham and promised to keep it. The law, which came four hundred thirty years later, cannot change that agreement and so destroy God's promise to Abraham. If the law could give us Abraham's blessing, then the promise would not be necessary. But that is not possible, because God freely gave his blessings to Abraham through the promise he had made.

So what was the law for? It was given to show that the wrong things people do are against God's will. And it continued until the special descendant, who had been promised, came. The law was given through angels who used Moses for a mediator to give the law to people. But a mediator is not needed when there is only one side, and God is only one.

Does this mean that the law is against God's promises? Never! That would be true only if the law could make us right. But God did not give a law that can bring life. Instead, the Scriptures showed that the whole world is bound by sin. This was so the promise would be given through faith to people who believe in Jesus Christ.

Before this faith came, we were all held prisoners by the law. We had no freedom until God showed us the way of faith that was coming. In other words, the law was our guardian leading us to Christ so that we could be made right with

God through faith. Now the way of faith has come, and we no longer live under a guardian.

You were all baptized into Christ, and so you were all clothed with Christ. This means that you are all children of God through faith in Christ Jesus. In Christ, there is no difference between Jew and Greek, slave and free person, male and female. You are all the same in Christ Jesus. You belong to Christ, so you are Abraham's descendants. You will inherit all of God's blessings because of the promise God made to Abraham.

Galatians 4:6-7 Since you are God's children, God sent the Spirit of his Son into your hearts, and the Spirit cries out, "Father." So now you are not a slave; you are God's child, and God will give you the blessing he promised, because you are his child.

Galatians 5:6 When we are in Christ Jesus, it is not important if we are circumcised or not. The important thing is faith—the kind of faith that works through love.

Matthew 14:29-31 Jesus said, "Come."

And Peter left the boat and walked on the water to Jesus. But when Peter saw the wind and the waves, he became afraid and began to sink. He shouted, "Lord, save me!"

Immediately Jesus reached out his hand and caught Peter. Jesus said, "Your faith is small. Why did you doubt?"

Pay Taxes?

Matthew 22:15-22 Then the Pharisees left that place and made plans to trap Jesus in saying something wrong. They sent some of their own followers and some people from the group called Herodians. They said, "Teacher, we know that you are an honest man and that you teach the truth about God's way. You are not afraid of what other people think about you, because you pay no attention to who they are. So tell us what you think. Is it right to pay taxes to Caesar or not?"

But knowing that these leaders were trying to trick him, Jesus said, "You hypocrites! Why are you trying to trap me? Show me a coin used for paying the tax." So the men showed him a coin. Then Jesus asked, "Whose image and name are on the coin?"

The men answered, "Caesar's."

Then Jesus said to them, "Give to Caesar the things that are Caesar's, and give to God the things that are God's."

When the men heard what Jesus said, they were amazed and left him and went away.

Mark 12:13-17 Same as above with variations.

Luke 20:20-26 Same as above with variations.

Matthew 17:24-27 When Jesus and his followers came to Capernaum, the men who collected the Temple tax came to Peter. They asked, "Does your teacher pay the Temple tax?"

Peter answered, "Yes, Jesus pays the tax."

Peter went into the house, but before he could speak, Jesus said to him, "What do you think? The kings of the earth collect different kinds of taxes. But who pays the taxes—the king's children or others?"

Peter answered, "Other people pay the taxes."

Jesus said to Peter, "Then the children of the king don't have to pay taxes. But we don't want to upset these tax collectors. So go to the lake and fish. After you catch the first fish, open its mouth and you will find a coin. Take that coin and give it to the tax collectors for you and me."

Romans 13:6-7 This is also why you pay taxes. Rulers are working for God and give their time to their work. Pay everyone, then, what you owe. If you owe any kind of tax, pay it. Show respect and honor to them all.

First Day Of The Week

Matthew 28:1-7 The day after the Sabbath day was the first day of the week. At dawn on the first day, Mary Magdalene and another woman named Mary went to look at the tomb.

At that time there was a strong earthquake. An angel of the Lord came down from heaven, went to the tomb, and rolled the stone away from the entrance. Then he sat on the stone. He was shining as bright as lightning, and his clothes were white as snow. The soldiers guarding the tomb shook with fear because of the angel, and they became like dead men.

The angel said to the women, "Don't be afraid. I know that you are looking for Jesus, who has been crucified. He is not here. He has risen from the dead as he said he would. Come and see the place where his body was. And go quickly and tell his followers, 'Jesus has risen from the dead. He is going into Galilee ahead of you, and you will see him there.'" Then the angel said, "Now I have told you."

John 20:19 When it was evening on the first day of the week, the followers were together. The doors were locked, because they were afraid of the Jews. Then Jesus came and stood right in the middle of them and said, "Peace be with you."

Acts 20:7 On the first day of the week, we all met together to break bread, and Paul spoke to the group. Because he was planning to leave the next day, he kept on talking until midnight.

1 Corinthians 16:2 On the first day of every week, each one of you should put aside money as you have been blessed. Save it up so you will not have to collect money after I come.

Revelation 1:10 On the Lord's day I was in the Spirit, and I heard a loud voice behind me that sounded like a trumpet.

Mark 16:9 After Jesus rose from the dead early on the first day of the week, he showed himself first to Mary Magdalene. One time in the past, he had forced seven demons out of her.

Luke 24:1 Very early on the first day of the week, at dawn, the women came to the tomb, bringing the spices they had prepared.

John 20:1-2 Early on the first day of the week, Mary Magdalene went to the tomb while it was still dark. When she saw that the large stone had been moved away from the tomb, she ran to Simon Peter and the follower whom Jesus loved. Mary said, "They have taken the Lord out of the tomb, and we don't know where they have put him."

The Sabbath Day

Luke 14:1-6 On a Sabbath day, when Jesus went to eat at the home of a leading Pharisee, the people were watching Jesus very closely. And in front of him was a man with dropsy. Jesus said to the Pharisees and experts on the law, "Is it right or wrong to heal on the Sabbath day?" But they would not answer his question. So Jesus took the man, healed him, and sent him away. Jesus said to the Pharisees and teachers of the law, "If your child or ox falls into a well on the Sabbath day, will you not pull him out quickly" And they could not answer him.

Luke 13: 10-17 Jesus was teaching in one of the synagogues on the Sabbath day. A woman was there who, for eighteen years, had an evil spirit in her that made her crippled. Her back was always bent; she could not stand up straight. When Jesus saw her, he called her over and said, "Woman, you are free from your sickness." Jesus put his hands on her, and immediately she was able to stand up straight and began praising God.

The synagogue leader was angry because Jesus healed on the Sabbath day. He said to the people, "There are six days when one has to work. So come to be healed on one of those days, and not on the Sabbath day."

The Lord answered, "You hypocrites! Doesn't each of you untie your work animals and lead them to drink water every day—even on the Sabbath day? This woman that I healed, a daughter of Abraham, has been held by Satan for eighteen years. Surely it is not wrong for her to be freed from her sickness on a Sabbath day!" When Jesus said this, all of those who were criticizing him were ashamed, but the entire crowd rejoiced at all the wonderful things Jesus was doing.

Matthew 12:1-13 At that time Jesus was walking through some fields of grain on a Sabbath day. His followers were hungry, so they began to pick the grain and eat it. When the Pharisees saw this, they said to Jesus, "Look! Your followers are doing what is unlawful to do on the Sabbath day."

Jesus answered, "Have you not read what David did when he and the people with him were hungry? He went into God's house, and he and those with him ate the holy bread, which was lawful only for priests to eat. And have you not read in the law of Moses that on every Sabbath day the priests in the Temple break this law about the Sabbath day? But the priests are not wrong for doing that. I tell you that there is something here that is greater than the Temple. The Scripture says, 'I want kindness more than I want animal sacrifices.' You don't really know what those words mean. If you understood them, you would not judge those who have done nothing wrong.

"So the Son of Man is Lord of the Sabbath day."

Jesus left there and went into their synagogue, where there was a man with a crippled hand. They were looking for a reason to accuse Jesus, so they asked him, "Is it right to heal on the Sabbath day?"

Jesus answered, "If any of you has a sheep, and it falls into a ditch on the Sabbath day, you will help it out of the ditch. Surely a human being is more important than a sheep. So it is lawful to do good things on the Sabbath day."

Then Jesus said to the man with the crippled hand, "Hold out your hand." The man held out his hand, and it became well again, like the other hand. But the Pharisees left and made plans to kill Jesus.

Mark 2:23-28 Same as above with variations.

Mark 3:1-6 Same as above with variations.

Luke 6:1-11 Same as above with variations.

Sabbath Day According To The Sabbath Day Believers

Luke 4:16 Jesus traveled to Nazareth, where he had grown up. On the Sabbath day he went to the synagogue, as he always did, and stood up to read.

Acts 17:2 Paul went into the synagogue as he always did, and on each Sabbath day for three weeks, he talked with the Jews about the Scriptures.

Acts 18:3-4 Because they were tentmakers, just as he was, he stayed with them and worked with them. Every Sabbath day he talked with the Jews and Greeks in the synagogue, trying to persuade them to believe in Jesus.

Acts 16:13 On the Sabbath day we went outside the city gate to the river where we thought we would find a special place for prayer. Some women had gathered there, so we sat down and talked with them.

Note: According to the Sabbath Day Believers (AKA SDB), the previous scriptures show that Jesus and Paul both observed the Sabbath day. SDB go on to say that keeping the Sabbath day holy was written in stone as part of the Ten Commandments. SDB claim that if this day had been changed, God or Jesus through the Scriptures would have made it known to us. SDB claim that the people who worship on Sunday say that they are under the new law or the Spirit of the law and not bound by special Jewish celebrations held on the Sabbath. SDB agree but state that man changed the day of worship to Sunday, not God. It was changed to Sunday by man to celebrate Christ's Resurrection. SDB claim that the Spirit of the law didn't change the Ten Commandments. They give an example: Jesus himself said that if you look at a women and want to sin sexually with her, in your mind, you have already done that sin with the woman. The spirit of the law didn't do away with the law against adultery. They go on to say that after Jesus was crucified on Friday, he observed the Sabbath by resting and waiting until Sunday to be Resurrected.

*Note: This writer believes that the Sabbath day was and is Jewish. **Exodus 31:16-17** "The Israelites must remember the Sabbath day as an agreement between them and me that will continue from now on. The Sabbath day will be a sign between me and the Israelites forever, because in six days I, the Lord, made the sky and the earth. On the seventh day I did not work; I rested."*

*This writer believes that Jesus is Lord even over the Sabbath day. Saul (Paul) who was converted by the resurrected Jesus writes in **Romans 1:5** "Through Christ, God gave me the special work of an apostle, which was to lead* *people of all nations to believe and obey. I do this work for him." Again Paul writes in* **Romans 1:16** *"I am proud of the Good News, because it is the power God uses to save everyone who believe—to save the Jews first, and also to save those who are not Jews." Paul, who brought Christianity to non-Jews, 1* **Timothy 2:7**, *would have been responsible for getting the day of worship right. Not only did he have the gift of the Holy Spirit, but he also had the power to heal and bring people back from the dead,* **Acts 20:9-12.** *In* **Acts 10:37-43** *Peter also had the power of the Holy Spirit to bring people back from the dead. If worshiping on Sunday and not the Sabbath was wrong, why didn't Jesus or the Holy Spirit give these early leaders corrective direction?*

Remember what Paul says in **Romans 14:5-8** *Some think that one day is more important than another, and others think every day is the same. Let all be sure in their own mind. Those who think one day is more important than other days are doing that for the Lord. And those who eat all kinds of food are doing that for the Lord, and they give thanks to God. Others who refuse to eat some foods do that for the Lord, and they give thanks to God. We do not live or die for ourselves. If we live, we are living for the Lord, and if we die, we are dying for the Lord. So living or dying, we belong to the Lord.*

Before Jesus Comes Again And How He Will Come

Matthew 24:1-51 As Jesus left the Temple and was walking away, his followers came up to show him the Temple's buildings. Jesus asked, "Do you see all these buildings? I tell you the truth, not one stone will be left on another. Every stone will be thrown down to the ground."

Later, as Jesus was sitting on the Mount of Olives, his followers came to be alone with him. They said, "Tell us, when will these things happen? And what will be the sign that it is time for you to come again and for this age to end?"

Jesus answered, "Be careful that no one fools you. Many will come in my name, saying, 'I am the Christ,' and they will fool many people. You will hear about wars and stories of wars that are coming, but don't be afraid. These thing must happen before the end comes. Nations will fight against other nations; kingdoms will fight against other kingdoms. There will be times when there is no food for people to eat, and there will be earthquakes in different places. These things are like the first pains when something new is about to be born.

"Then people will arrest you, hand you over to be hurt, and kill you. They will hate you because you believe in me. At that time, many will lose their faith, and they will turn against each other and hate each other. Many false prophets will come and cause many people to believe lies. There will be more and more evil in the world, so most people will stop showing their love for each other. But those people who keep their faith until the end will be saved. **The Good News about God's kingdom will be preached in all the world, to every nation. Then the end will come.**

"Daniel the prophet spoke about the 'destroying terror.' You will see this standing in the holy place." (You who read this should understand what it means.) "At that time, the people in Judea should run away to the mountains. If people are on the roofs of their houses, they must not go down to get anything out of their houses. If people are in the fields, they must not go back to get their coats. At that time, how terrible it will be for women who are pregnant or have nursing babies! Pray that it will not be winter or a Sabbath day when these things happen and you have to run away, because at that time there will be much trouble. There will be more trouble than there has ever been since the beginning of the world until now, and nothing as bad will ever happen again. God has decided to make that terrible time short. Otherwise, no one would go on living. But God will make that time short to help the people he has chosen. At that time, someone might say to you, 'Look, there is the Christ!' Or another person might say, 'There he is!' But don't believe them. **False Christs and false prophets will come and perform great wonders and miracles. They will try to fool even the people God has chosen, if that is possible**. Now I have warned you about this before it happens.

"If people tell you, 'The Christ is in the desert,' don't go there. If they say, 'The Christ is in the inner room,' don't believe it. **When the Son of Man comes, he will be seen by everyone, like lightning flashing from the east to the west**. Wherever the dead body is, there the vultures will gather.

> "Soon after the trouble of those days,
> 'the sun will grow dark,
> and the moon will not give its light.
> The stars will fall from the sky.
> And the powers of heavens will be shaken.' (Isaiah 13:10; 34:4)

"At that time, the sign of the Son of Man will appear in the sky. Then all the peoples of the world will cry. They will see the Son of Man coming on clouds in the sky with great power and glory. He will use a loud trumpet to send his angels all around the earth, and they will gather his chosen people from every part of the world.

"Learn a lesson from the fig tree: When its branches become green and soft and new leaves appear, you know summer is near. In the same way, when you see all these things happening, you will know that the time is near, ready to come. I tell you the truth, all these things will happen while the people of this time are still living. Earth and sky will be destroyed, but the words I have said will never be destroyed.

"No one knows when that day or time will be, not the angels in heaven, not even the Son. Only the Father knows. When the Son of Man comes, it will be like what happened during Noah's time. In those days before the flood, people were eating and drinking, marrying and giving their children to be marred, until the day Noah entered the boat. They knew nothing about what was happening until the flood came and destroyed them. It will be the same when the Son of Man comes. Two men will be in the field. One will be taken, and the other will be left. Two women will be grinding grain with a mill. One will be taken, and the other will be left.

"So always be ready, because you don't know the day your Lord will come. Remember this: If the owner of the house knew what time of night a thief was coming, the owner would watch and not let the thief break in. So you also must be ready, because the Son of Man will come at a time you don't expect him.

"Who is the wise and loyal servant that the master trusts to give the other servants their food at the right time? When the master comes and finds the servant doing his work, the servant will be blessed. I tell you the truth, the master will choose that servant to take care of everything he owns. But suppose that evil servant thinks to himself, 'My master will not come back soon,' and he begins to beat the other servants and eat and get drunk with others like him? The master will come when that servant is not ready and is not expecting him. Then the master will cut him in pieces and send him away to be with the hypocrites, where people will cry and grind their teeth with pain."

Mark 13:3-37 Same as above with variations.

..."You must be careful. People will arrest you and take you to court and beat you in their synagogues. You will be forced to stand before kings and governors, to tell them about me. This will happen to you because you follow me....

"Brothers will give their own brothers to be killed, and fathers will give their own children to be killed. Children will fight against their own parents and cause them to be put to death. All people will hate you because you follow me, but those people who keep their faith until the end will be saved...."

Luke 17:24-37 Same as above with variations.

..."When the Son of Man comes again, he will shine like lightning, which flashes across the sky and lights it up from one side to the other....It will be the same as during the time of Lot. People were eating, drinking, buying, selling, planting, and building. But the day Lot left Sodom, fire and sulfur rained down from the sky and killed them all. This is how it will be when the Son of Man comes again....

"A person who is in the field should not go back home. Remember Lot's wife. Those who try to keep their lives will lose them. But those who give up their lives will save them. I tell you, on that night two people will be sleeping in one bed; one will be taken and the other will be left. There will be two women grinding grain together; one will be taken, and the other will be left."

The followers asked Jesus, "Where will this be, Lord?"

Jesus answered, "Where there is a dead body, there the vultures will gather."

Luke 21:5-36 Same as above with variations.

..."When you see armies all around Jerusalem, you will know it will soon be destroyed. At that time, the people in Judea should run away to the mountains. The people in Jerusalem must get out, and those who are near the city should not go in. These are the days of punishment to bring about all that is written in the Scriptures. How terrible it will be for women who are pregnant or have nursing babies! Great trouble will come upon this land, and God will be angry with these people. They will be killed by the sword and taken as prisoners to all nations. Jerusalem will be crushed by non-Jewish people until their time is over.

"There will be signs in the sun, moon, and stars. On earth, nations will be afraid and confused because of the roar and fury of the sea. People will be so afraid they will faint, wondering what is happening to the world, because the powers of the heavens will be shaken. Then people will see the Son of Man coming in a cloud with power and great glory. When these things begin to happen, look up and hold your heads high, because the time when God will free you is near!"

..."Be careful not to spend your time feasting, drinking, or worrying about worldly things. If you do, that day might come on you suddenly, like a trap on all people on earth. So be ready all the time. Pray that you will be strong enough to escape all these things that will happen and that you will be able to stand before the Son of Man."

Luke 23:27-31 A large crowd of people was following Jesus, including some women who were sad and crying for him. But Jesus turned and said to them, "Women of Jerusalem, don't cry for me. Cry for yourselves and for your children. The time is coming when people will say, 'Happy are the women who cannot have children and who have no babies to nurse.' Then people will say to the mountains, 'Fall on us!' And they will say to the hills, 'Cover us!' If they act like this now when life is good, what will happen when bad times come?"

1 Corinthians 15:23-28 But everyone will be raised to life in the right order. Christ was first to be raised. When Christ comes again, those who belong to him will be raised to life, and then the end will come. At that time Christ will destroy all rulers, authorities, and powers, and he will hand over the kingdom to God the Father. Christ must rule until he puts all enemies under his control. The last enemy to be destroyed will be death. The **Scripture says that God put all things under his control. When it says "all things" are under him, it is clear this does not include God himself. God is the One who put everything under his control. After everything has been put under the Son, then he will put himself under God, who had put all things under him. Then God will be the complete ruler over everything.**

1 Thessalonians 4:13-18 Brothers and sisters, we want you to know about those Christians who have died so you will not be sad, as others who have no hope. We believe that Jesus died and that he rose again. So, because of him, God will raise with Jesus those who have died. What we tell you now is the Lord's own message. We who are living when the Lord comes again will not go before those who have already died. The Lord himself will come down from heaven with a loud command, with the voice of the archangel, and with the trumpet call of God. And those who have died believing in Christ will rise first. After that, we who are still alive will be gathered up with them in the clouds to meet the Lord in the air. And we will be with the Lord forever. So encourage each other with these words.

1 Thessalonians 5:1-11 Now, brothers and sisters, we do not need to write you about times and dates. You know very well that the day the Lord comes again will be a surprise, life a thief that comes in the night. While people are saying, "We have peace and we are safe," they will be destroyed quickly. It is like pains that come quickly to a woman having a baby. Those people will not escape. But you, brothers and sisters, are not living in darkness, and so that day will not surprise you like a thief. You are all people who belong to the light and to the day. We do not belong to the night or to darkness. So we should not be like other people who are sleeping, but we should be alert and have self-control. Those who sleep, sleep at night. Those who get drunk, get drunk at night. But we belong to the day, so we should control ourselves. We should wear faith and love to protect us, and the hope of salvation should be our helmet. God did not choose us to suffer his anger but to have salvation through our Lord Jesus Christ. Jesus died for us so that we can live together with him, whether we are alive or dead when he comes. So encourage each other and give each other strength, just as you are doing now.

2 Thessalonians 1:7-10 And he will give rest to you who are troubled and to us also when the Lord Jesus appears with burning fire from heaven with his powerful angels. Then he will punish those who do not know God and who do not obey the Good News about our Lord Jesus Christ. Those people will be punished with a destruction that continues forever. They will be kept away from the Lord and from his great power. This will happen on the day when the Lord Jesus comes to receive glory because of his holy people. And all the people who have believed will be amazed at Jesus. You will be in that group, because you believed what we told you.

2 Thessalonians 2:1-12 Brothers and sisters, we have something to say about the coming of our Lord Jesus Christ and the time when we will meet together with him. Do not become easily upset in your thinking or afraid if you hear that the day of the Lord has already come. Someone may say this in a prophecy or in a message or in a letter as if it came from us. Do not let anyone fool you in any way. That day of the Lord will not come until the turning away from God happens and the Man of Evil, who is on his way to hell, appears. He will be against and put himself above anything called God or anything that people worship. And that Man of Evil will even go into God's Temple and sit there and say that he is God.

I told you when I was with you that all this would happen. Do you not remember? And now you know what is stopping that Man of Evil so he will appear at the right time. The secret power of evil is already working in the world, but there is one who is stopping that power. And he will continue to stop it until he is taken out of the way. Then that Man of Evil will appear, and the Lord Jesus will kill him with the breath that comes from his mouth and will destroy him with the glory of his coming. The Man of Evil will come by the power of

Satan. He will have great power, and he will do many different false miracles, signs, and wonders. He will use every kind of evil to trick those who are lost. They will die, because they refused to love the truth. (If they loved the truth, they would be saved.) For this reason God sends them something powerful that leads them away from the truth so they will believe a lie. So all those will be judged guilty who did not believe the truth, but enjoyed doing evil.

1 Timothy 4:1-5 Now the Holy Spirit clearly says that in the later times some people will stop believing the faith. They will follow spirits that lie and teachings of demons. Such teachings come from the false words of liars whose consciences are destroyed as if by a hot iron. They forbid people to marry and tell them not to eat certain foods which God created to be eaten with thanks by people who believe and know the truth. Everything God made is good, and nothing should be refused if it is accepted with thanks, because it is made holy by what God has said and by prayer.

2 Timothy 3:1-6 Remember this! In the last days there will be many troubles, because people will love themselves, love money, brag, and be proud. They will say evil things against others and will not obey their parents or be thankful or be the kind of people God wants. They will not love others, will refuse to forgive, will gossip, and will not control themselves. They will be cruel, will hate what is good, will turn against their friends, and will do foolish things without thinking. They will be conceited, will love pleasure instead of God, and will act as if they serve God but will not have his power. Stay away from those people. Some of them go into homes and get control of silly women who are full of sin and are led by many evil desires. These women are always learning new teachings, but they are never able to understand the truth fully. Just as Jannes and Jambres were against Moses, these people are against the truth. Their thinking has been ruined, and they have failed in trying to follow the faith. But they will not be successful in what they do, because as with Jannes and Jambres, everyone will see that they are foolish.

2 Peter 3:3-9 It is most important for you to understand what will happen in the last days. People will laugh at you. They will live doing the evil things they want to do. They will say, "Jesus promised to come again. Where is he? Our fathers have died, but the world continues the way it has been since it was made." But they do not want to remember what happened long ago. By the word of God heaven was made, and the earth was made from water and with water. Then the world was flooded and destroyed with water. And that same word of God is keeping heaven and earth that we now have in order to be destroyed by fire. They are being kept for the Judgment Day and the destruction of all who are against God.

But do not forget this one thing, dear friends: To the Lord one day is as a thousand years, and a thousand years is as one day. The Lord is not slow in doing what he promised—the way some people understand slowness. But God is being patient with you. He does not want anyone to be lost, but he wants all people to change their hearts and lives.

2 Peter 3:10-14 But the day of the Lord will come like a thief. The skies will disappear with a loud noise. Everything in them will be destroyed by fire, and the earth and everything in it will be burned up. In that way everything will be destroyed. So what kind of people should you be? You should live holy lives and serve God, as you wait for and look forward to the coming of the day of God. When that day comes, the skies will be destroyed with fire, and everything in them will melt with heat. But God made a promise to us, and we are waiting for a new heaven and a new earth where goodness lives.

Dear friends, since you are waiting for this to happen, do your best to be without sin and without fault. Try to be at peace with God.

Jude 17-19 Dear friends, remember what the apostles of our Lord Jesus Christ said before. They said to you, "In the last times there will be people who laugh about God, following their own evil desires which are against God." These are the people who divide you, people whose thoughts are only of this world, who do not have the Spirit.

The Lord's Supper

Matthew 26:26-30 While they were eating, Jesus took some bread and thanked God for it and broke. Then he gave it to his followers and said, "Take this bread and eat it; this is my body."

Then Jesus took a cup and thanked God for it and gave it to the followers. He said, "Every one of you drink this. This is my blood which is the new agreement that God makes with his people. This blood is poured out for many to forgive their sins. I tell you this: I will not drink of this fruit of the vine again until that day when I drink it new with you in my Father's kingdom."

After singing a hymn, they went out to the Mount of Olives.

Mark 14:22-26 Same as above with variations.

Luke 22:14-20 When the time came, Jesus and the apostles were sitting at the table. He said to them, "I wanted very much to eat this Passover meal with you before I suffer. I will not eat another Passover meal until it is given its true meaning in the kingdom of God."

Then Jesus took a cup, gave thanks, and said, "Take this cup and share it among yourselves. I will not drink again from the fruit of the vine until God's kingdom comes."

Then Jesus took some bread, gave thanks, broke it, and gave it to the apostles, saying, "This is my body, which I am giving for you. Do this to remember me." In the same way, after supper, Jesus took the cup and said, "This cup is the new agreement that God makes with his people. This new agreement begins with my blood which is poured out for you."

Acts 2:42 They spent their time learning the apostles' teaching, sharing, breaking bread, and praying together.

Acts 20:7 On the first day of the week, we all met together to break bread, and Paul spoke to the group. Because he was planning to leave the next day, he kept on talking until midnight.

1 Corinthians 10:16-17 We give thanks for the cup of blessing, which is a sharing in the blood of Christ. And the bread that we break is a sharing in the body of Christ. Because there is one loaf of bread, we who are many are one body, because we all share that one loaf.

1 Corinthians 11:23-34 The teaching I gave you is the same teaching I received from the Lord: On the night when the Lord Jesus was handed over to be killed, he took bread and gave thanks for it. Then he broke the bread and said,

"This is my body; it is for you. Do this to remember me." In the same way, after they ate, Jesus took the cup. He said, "This cup is the new agreement that is sealed with the blood of my death. When you drink this, do it to remember me." Every time you eat this bread and drink this cup you are telling others about the Lord's death until he comes.

So a person who eats the bread or drinks the cup of the Lord in a way that is not worthy of it will be guilty of sinning against the body and the blood of the Lord. Look into your own hearts before you eat the bread and drink the cup, because all who eat the bread and drink the cup without recognizing the body eat and drink judgment against themselves. That is why many in your group are sick and weak, and many have died. But if we judged ourselves in the right way, God would not judge us. But when the Lord judges us, he punishes us so that we will not be destroyed along with the world.

So my brothers and sisters, when you come together to eat, wait for each other. Anyone who is too hungry should eat at home so that in meeting together you will not bring God's judgment on yourselves. I will tell you what to do about the other things when I come.

Jesus Foretells Of His Crucifixion

Mark 8:31-33 Then Jesus began to teach them that the Son of Man must suffer many things and that he would be rejected by the older Jewish leaders, the leading priests, and the teachers of the law. He told them that the Son of Man must be killed and then rise from the dead after three days. Jesus told them plainly what would happen. Then Peter took Jesus aside and began to tell him not to talk like that. But Jesus turned and looked at his followers. Then he told Peter not to talk that way. He said, "Go away from me, Satan! You don't care about the things of God, but only about things people think are important."

Mark 9:30-32 Then Jesus and his followers left that place and went through Galilee. He didn't want anyone to know where he was, because he was teaching his followers. He said to them, "The Son of Man will be handed over to people, and they will kill him. After three days, he will rise from the dead." But the followers did not understand what Jesus meant, and they were afraid to ask him.

Mark 10:33-34 He said, "Look, we are going to Jerusalem. The Son of Man will be turned over to the leading priests and the teachers of the law. They will say that he must die, and they will turn him over to the non-Jewish people, who will laugh at him and spit on him. They will beat him with whips and crucify him. But on the third day, he will rise to life again."

Luke 9:22 "The Son of Man must suffer many things. He will be rejected by the older Jewish leaders, the leading priests, and the teachers of the law. He will be killed and after three days will be raised from the dead."

Luke 9:43-45 All the people were amazed at the great power of God.
While everyone was wondering about all that Jesus did, he said to his followers, "Don't forget what I tell you now: The Son of Man will be handed over to people." But the followers did not understand what this meant; the meaning was hidden from them so they could not understand. But they were afraid to ask Jesus about it.

Luke 13:31-35 At that time some Pharisees came to Jesus and said, "Go away from here! Herod wants to kill you!"
Jesus said to them, "Go tell that fox Herod, 'Today and tomorrow I am forcing demons out and healing people. Then, on the third day, I will reach my goal.' Yet I must be on my way today and tomorrow and the next day. Surely it cannot be right for a prophet to be killed anywhere except in Jerusalem.

"Jerusalem, Jerusalem! You kill the prophets and stone to death those who are sent to you. Many times I wanted to gather your people as a hen gathers her chicks under her wings, but you would not let me. Now your house is left completely empty. I tell you, you will not see me until that time when you will say, 'God bless the One who comes in the name of the Lord.'"

Luke 18:31-34 Then Jesus took the twelve apostles aside and said to them, "We are going to Jerusalem. Everything the prophets wrote about the Son of Man will happen. He will be turned over to those who are not Jews. They will laugh at him, insult him, spit on him, beat him with whips, and kill him. But on the third day, he will rise to life again." The apostles did not understand this; the meaning was hidden from them, and they did not realize what was said.

Luke 22:35-45 Then Jesus said to the apostles, "When I sent you out without a purse, a bag, or sandals, did you need anything?"
They said, "No."
He said to them, "But now if you have a purse or a bag, carry that with you. If you don't have a sword, sell your coat and buy one. The Scripture says, 'He was treated like a criminal,' and I tell you this scripture must have its full meaning. It was written about me, and it is happening now."
His followers said, "Look, Lord, here are two swords."
He said to them, "That is enough."
Jesus left the city and went to the Mount of Olives, as he often did, and his followers went with him. When he reached the place, he said to them, "Pray for strength against temptation."
Then Jesus went about a stone's throw away from them. He kneeled down and prayed, "Father, if you are willing, take away this cup of suffering. But do what you want, not what I want." Then an angel from heaven appeared to him to strengthen him. Being full of pain, Jesus prayed even harder. His sweat was like drops of blood falling to the ground. When he finished praying, he went to his followers and found them asleep because of their sadness. Jesus said to them, "Why are you sleeping? Get up and pray for strength against temptation."

Matthew 12:38-42 Then some of the Pharisees and teachers of the law answered Jesus, saying, "Teacher, we want to see you work a miracle as a sign."
Jesus answered, "Evil and sinful people are the ones who want to see a miracle for a sign. But no sign will be given to them, except the sign of the prophet Jonah. Jonah was in the stomach of the big fish for three days and three nights. In the same way, the Son of Man will be in the grave three days and three nights. On the Judgment Day the people from Nineveh will stand up with you people who live now, and they will show that you are guilty. When Jonah preached to them, they were sorry and changed their lives. And I tell you that

someone greater than Jonah is here. On the Judgment Day, the Queen of the South will stand up with you people who live today. She will show that you are guilty, because she came from far away to listen to Solomon's wise teaching. And I tell you that someone greater than Solomon is here."

True Giving

Mark 12:41-44 Jesus sat near the Temple money box and watched the people put in their money. Many rich people gave large sums of money. Then a poor widow came and put in two small copper coins, which were only worth a few cents.

Calling his followers to him, Jesus said, "I tell you the truth, this poor widow gave more than all those rich people. They gave only what they did not need. This woman is very poor, but she gave all she had; she gave all she had to live on."

Luke 21:1-4 Same as above with variations.

Luke 12:32-34 "Don't fear, little flock, because your Father wants to give you the kingdom. Sell your possessions and give to the poor. Get for yourselves purses that will not wear out, the treasure in heaven that never runs out, where thieves can't steal and moths can't destroy. Your heart will be where your treasure is."

2 Corinthians 9:6-9 Remember this: The person who plants a little will have a small harvest, but the person who plants a lot will have a big harvest. Each one should give as you have decided in your heart to give. You should not be sad when you give, and you should not give because you feel forced to give. God loves the person who gives happily. And God can give you more blessings than you need. Then you will always have plenty of everything—enough to give to every good work. It is written in the Scriptures:

"He gives freely to the poor.

The things he does are right and will continue forever." (Psalm 112:9)

Those Who Are Forgiven Of Many Sins Will Show Great Love

Luke 7:36-50 One of the Pharisees asked Jesus to eat with him, so Jesus went into the Pharisee's house and sat at the table. A sinful woman in the town learned that Jesus was eating at the Pharisee's house. So she brought an alabaster jar of perfume and stood behind Jesus at his feet, crying. She began to wash his feet with her tears, and she dried them with her hair, kissing them many times and rubbing them with the perfume. When the Pharisee who asked Jesus to come to his house saw this, he thought to himself, "If Jesus were a prophet, he would know that the woman touching him is a sinner!"

Jesus said to the Pharisee, "Simon, I have something to say to you."

Simon said, "Teacher, tell me."

Jesus said, "Two people owed money to the same banker. One owed five hundred coins and the other owed fifty. They had no money to pay what they owed, but the banker told both of them they did not have to pay him. Which person will love the banker more?"

Simon, the Pharisee, answered, "I think it would be the one who owed him the most money."

Jesus said to Simon, "You are right." Then Jesus turned toward the woman and said to Simon, "Do you see this woman? When I came into your house, you gave me no water for my feet, but she washed my feet with her tears and dried them with her hair. You gave me no kiss of greeting, but she has been kissing my feet since I came in. You did not put oil on my head, but she poured perfume on my feet. I tell you that her many sins are forgiven, so she showed great love. But the person who is forgiven only a little will love only a little."

Then Jesus said to her, "Your sins are forgiven."

The people sitting at the table began to say among themselves, "Who is this who even forgives sins?"

Jesus said to the woman, "Because you believed, you are saved from your sins. Go in peace."

Luke 15:1-10 The tax collectors and sinners all came to listen to Jesus. But the Pharisees and the teachers of the law began to complain: "Look, this man welcomes sinners and even eats with them."

Then Jesus told them this story: "Suppose one of you has a hundred sheep but loses one of them. Then he will leave the other ninety-nine sheep in the open field and go out and look for the lost sheep until he finds it. And when he finds it, he happily puts it on his shoulders and goes home. He calls to his friends and neighbors and says, 'Be happy with me because I found my lost sheep.' In the same way, I tell you there is more joy in heaven over one sinner who changes his heart and life, than over ninety-nine good people who don't need to change.

"Suppose a woman has ten silver coins, but loses one. She will light a lamp, sweep the house, and look carefully for the coin until she finds it. And when she finds it, she will call her friends and neighbors and say, 'Be happy with me because I have found the coin that I lost.' In the same way, there is joy in the presence of the angels of God when one sinner changes his heart and life."

Luke 15:11-32 (The story of the prodigal son) Then Jesus said, "A man had two sons. The younger son said to his father, 'Give me my share of the property.' So the father divided the property between his two sons. Then the younger son gathered up all that was his and traveled far away to another country. There he wasted his money in foolish living. After he had spent everything, a time came when there was no food anywhere in the country, and the son was poor and hungry. So he got a job with one of the citizens there who sent the son into the fields to feed pigs. The son was so hungry that he wanted to eat the pods the pigs were eating, but no one gave him anything. When he realized what he was doing, he thought, 'All of my father's servants have plenty of food. But I am here, almost dying with hunger. I will leave and return to my father and say to him, "Father, I have sinned against God and have done wrong to you. I am no longer worthy to be called your son, but let me be like one of your servants."' So the son left and went to his father.

"While the son was still a long way off, his father saw him and felt sorry for his son. So the father ran to him and hugged and kissed him. The son said, 'Father, I have sinned against God and have done wrong to you. I am no longer worthy to be called your son.' But the father said to his servants, 'Hurry! Bring the best clothes and put them on him. Also, put a ring on his finger and sandals on his feet. And get our fat calf and kill it so we can have a feast and celebrate. My son was dead, but now he is alive again! He was lost, but now he is found!' So they began to celebrate.

"The older son was in the field, and as he came closer to the house, he heard the sound of music and dancing. So he called to one of the servants and asked what all this meant. The servant said, 'Your brother has come back, and your father killed the fat calf, because your brother came home safely.' The older son was angry and would not go in to the feast. So his father went out and begged him to come in. But the older son said to his father, 'I have served you like a slave for many years and have always obeyed your commands. But you never gave me even a young goat to have at a feast with my friends. But your other son, who wasted all your money on prostitutes, comes home, and you kill the fat calf for him!' The father said to him, 'Son, you are always with me, and all that I have is yours. We had to celebrate and be happy because your brother was dead, but now he is alive. He was lost, but now he is found.'"

Luke 18:9-14 Jesus told this story to some people who thought they were very good and looked down on everyone else: "A Pharisee and a tax collector both went to the Temple to pray. The Pharisee stood alone and prayed, 'God, I thank you that I am not like other people who steal, cheat, or take part in adultery, or even like this tax collector. I give up eating twice a week, and I give one-tenth of everything I get!'

"The tax collector, standing at a distance, would not even look up to heaven. But he beat on his chest because he was so sad. He said, 'God, have mercy on me, a sinner.' I tell you, when this man went home, he was right with God, but the Pharisee was not. All who make themselves great will be made humble, but all who make themselves humble will be made great."

Bad Things Happen To Good People

Luke 13:1-5 At that time some people were there who told Jesus that Pilate had killed some people from Galilee while they were worshiping. He mixed their blood with the blood of the animals they were sacrificing to God. Jesus answered, "Do you think this happened to them because they were more sinful than all others from Galilee? No, I tell you. But unless you change your hearts and lives, you will be destroyed as they were! What about those eighteen people who died when the tower of Siloam fell on them? Do you think they were more sinful than all the others who live in Jerusalem? No, I tell you. But unless you change your hearts and lives, you will all be destroyed too!"

John 9:1-5 As Jesus was walking along, he saw a man who had been born blind. His followers asked him, "Teacher, whose sin caused this man to be born blind—his own sin or his parent's sin?"

Jesus answered, "It is not this man's sin or his parents' sin that made him be blind. This man was born blind so that God's power could be shown in him. While it is daytime, we must continue doing the work of the One who sent me. Night is coming, when no one can work. While I am in the world, I am the light of the world."

John 9:26-34 They asked, "What did he do to you? How did he make you see again?"

He answered, "I already told you, and you didn't listen. Why do you want to hear it again? Do you want to become his followers, too?"

Then they insulted him and said, "You are his follower, but we are followers of Moses. We know that God spoke to Moses, but we don't even know where this man comes from."

The man answered, "This is a very strange thing. You don't know where he comes from, and yet he opened my eyes. We all know that God does not listen to sinners, but he listens to anyone who worships and obeys him. Nobody has ever heard of anyone giving sight to man born blind. If this man were not from God, he could do nothing."

They answered, "You were born full of sin! Are you trying to teach us?" And they threw him out.

James 1:2-3 My brothers and sisters, when you have many kinds of troubles, you should be full of joy, because you know that these troubles test your faith, and this will give you patience.

1 Peter 1:5-9 God's power protects you through your faith until salvation is shown to you at the end of time. This makes you very happy, even though now for a short time different kinds of troubles may make you sad. These troubles come to prove that your faith is pure. This purity of faith is worth more than gold, which can be proved to be pure by fire but will ruin. But the purity of your faith will bring you praise and glory and honor when Jesus Christ is shown to you. You have not seen Christ, but still you love him. You cannot see him now, but you believe in him. So you are filled with a joy that cannot be explained, a joy full of glory. And you are receiving the goal of your faith—the salvation of your souls.

Romans 5:3-5 We also have joy with our troubles, because we know that these troubles produce patience. And patience produces character, and character produces hope. And this hope will never disappoint us, because God has poured out his love to fill our hearts. He gave us his love through the Holy Spirit, whom God has given to us.

1 Peter 4:12-13 My friends, do not be surprised at the terrible trouble which now comes to test you. Do not think that something strange is happening to you. But be happy that you are sharing in Christ's sufferings so that you will be happy and full of joy when Christ comes again in glory.

Romans 8:17-18 If we are God's children, we will receive blessings from God together with Christ. But we must suffer as Christ suffered so that we will have glory as Christ has glory.

The sufferings we have now are nothing compared to the great glory that will be shown to us.

Who Will Be Saved?

Luke 13:22-30 Jesus was teaching in every town and village as he traveled toward Jerusalem. Someone said to Jesus, "Lord, will only a few people be saved?"

Jesus said, "Try hard to enter through the narrow door, because many people will try to enter there, but they will not be able. When the owner of the house gets up and closes the door, you can stand outside and knock on the door and say, 'Sir, open the door for us.' But he will answer, 'I don't know you or where you come from.' Then you will say, 'We ate and drank with you, and you taught in the streets of our town.' But he will say to you, 'I don't know you or where you come from. Go away from me, all you who do evil!' You will cry and grind your teeth with pain when you see Abraham, Isaac, Jacob, and all the prophets in God's kingdom, but you yourselves thrown outside. People will come from the east, west, north, and south and will sit down at the table in the kingdom of God. There are those who have the lowest place in life now who will have the highest place in the future. And there are those who have the highest place now who will have the lowest place in the future."

Luke 14:15-24 One of those at the table with Jesus heard these things and said to him, "Happy are the people who will share in the meal in God's kingdom."

Jesus said to him, "A man gave a big banquet and invited many people. When it was time to eat, the man sent his servant to tell the guests, 'Come. Everything is ready.'

But all the guests made excuses. The first one said, 'I have just bought a field, and I must go look at it. Please excuse me.' Another said, 'I have just bought five pairs of oxen; I must go and try them. Please excuse me.' A third person said, 'I just got married; I can't come.' So the servant returned and told his master what had happened. Then the master became angry and said, 'Go at once into the streets and alleys of the town, and bring in the poor, the crippled, the blind, and the lame.' Later the servant said to him, 'Master, I did what you commanded, but we still have room.' The master said to the servant, 'Go out to the roads and country lanes, and urge the people there to come so my house will be full. I tell you, none of those whom I invited first will eat with me.'"

Luke 14:25-33 Large crowds were traveling with Jesus, and he turned and said to them, "If anyone comes to me but loves his father, mother, wife, children, brothers, or sisters—or even life—more than me, he cannot be my follower. Whoever is not willing to carry the cross and follow me cannot be my follower. If you want to build a tower, you first sit down and decide how much it will cost, to see if you have enough money to finish the job. If you don't, you might lay the foundation, but you would not be able to finish. Then all who would see it would make fun of you, saying, 'This person began to build but was not able to finish.'

"If a king is going to fight another king, first he will sit down and plan. He will decide if he and his ten thousand soldiers can defeat the other king who has twenty thousand soldiers. If he can't, then while the other kings is still far away, he will send some people to speak to him and ask for peace. In the same way, you must give up everything you have to be my follower."

Luke 16: 19-31 (The rich man and Lazarus) Jesus said, "There was a rich man who always dressed in the finest clothes and lived in luxury every day. And a very poor man named Lazarus, whose body was covered with sores, was laid at the rich man's gate. He wanted to eat only the small pieces of food that fell from the rich man's table. And the dogs would come and lick his sores. Later, Lazarus died, and the angels carried him to the arms of Abraham. The rich man died, too, and was buried. In the place of the dead, he was in much pain. The rich man saw Abraham far away with Lazarus at his side. He called, 'Father Abraham, have mercy on me! Send Lazarus to dip his finger in water and cool my tongue, because I am suffering in this fire!' But Abraham said, 'Child, remember when you were alive you had the good things in life, but bad things happened to Lazarus. Now he is comforted here, and you are suffering. Besides, there is a big pit between you and us, so no one can cross over to you, and no one can leave there and come here.' The rich man said, 'Father, then please send Lazarus to my father's house. I have five brothers, and Lazarus could warn them so that they will not come to this place of pain.' But Abraham said, 'They have the law of Moses and the writings of the prophets; let them learn from them.' The rich man said, 'No, father Abraham! If someone goes to them from the dead, they would believe and change their hearts and lives.' But Abraham said to him, 'If they will not listen to Moses and the prophets, they will not listen to someone who comes back from the dead.'"

Luke 18:15-17 Some people brought even their babies to Jesus so he could touch them. When the followers saw this, they told them to stop. But Jesus called for the children, saying, "Let the little children come to me. Don't stop them, because the kingdom of God belongs to people who are like these children. I tell you the truth, you must accept the kingdom of God as if you were a child, or you will never enter it."

Luke 18:24-30 Jesus looked at him and said, "It is very hard for rich people to enter the kingdom of God. It is easier for a camel to go through the eye of a needle than for a rich person to enter the kingdom of God."

When the people heard this, they asked, "Then who can be saved?"

Jesus answered, "God can do things that are not possible for people to do."

Peter said, "Look, we have left everything and followed you."

Jesus said, "I tell you the truth, all those who have left houses, wives, brothers, parents, or children for the kingdom of God will get much more in this life. And in the age that is coming, they will have life forever."

Luke 18:35-43 As Jesus came near the city of Jericho, a blind man was sitting beside the road, begging. When he heard the people coming down the road, he asked, "What is happening?"

They told him, **"Jesus, from Nazareth, is going by."**

The blind man cried out, "Jesus, Son of David, have mercy on me!"

The people leading the group warned the blind man to be quiet. But the blind man shouted even more. "Son of David, have mercy on me!"

Jesus stopped and ordered the blind man to be brought to him. When he came near, Jesus asked him, "What do you want me to do for you?"

He said, "Lord, I want to see."

Jesus said to him, "Then see. You are healed because you believed."

At once the man was able to see, and he followed Jesus, thanking God. All the people who saw this praised God.

1 Peter 3:19-22 And in the spirit he went and preached to the spirits in prison who refused to obey God long ago in the time of Noah. God was waiting patiently for them while Noah was building the boat. Only a few people—eight in all—were saved by water. And that water is like baptism that now saves you—not the washing of dirt from the body, but the promise made to God from a good conscience. And this is because Jesus Christ was raised from the dead. Now Jesus has gone into heaven and is at God's right side ruling over angels, authorities, and powers.

1 Peter 4:16-19 But if you suffer because you are a Christian, do not be ashamed. Praise God because you wear that name. It is time for judgment to begin with God's family. And if that judging begins with us, what will happen to those people who do not obey the Good News of God?

"If it is very hard for a good person to be saved,

the wicked person and the sinner will surely be lost!" (Proverbs 3:34)

So those who suffer as God wants should trust their souls to the faithful Creator as they continue to do what is right.

Matthew 22:14 "Yes, many people are invited, but only a few are chosen."

Luke 10:25-37 (The Good Samaritan) Then an expert on the law stood up to test Jesus, saying, "Teacher, what must I do to get life forever?"

Jesus said, "What is written in the law? What do you read there?"

The man answered, "Love the Lord your God with all your heart, all your soul, all your strength, and all your mind." Also, "Love your neighbor as you love yourself."

Jesus said to him, "Your answer is right. Do this and you will live."

But the man, wanting to show the importance of his question, said to Jesus, "And who is my neighbor?"

Jesus answered, "As a man was going down from Jerusalem to Jericho, some robbers attacked him. They tore off his clothes, beat him, and left him lying there, almost dead. It happened that a Jewish priest was going down that road. When he saw the man, he walked by on the other side. Next, a Levite came there, and after he went over and looked at the man, he walked by on the other side of the road. Then a Samaritan traveling down the road came to where the hurt man was. When he saw the man, he felt very sorry for him. The Samaritan went to him, poured olive oil and wine on his wounds, and bandaged them. Then he put the hurt man on his own donkey and took him to an inn where he cared for him. The next day, the Samaritan brought out two coins, gave them to the innkeeper, and said, 'Take care of this man. If you spend more money on him, I will pay it back to you when I come again.'"

Then Jesus said, "Which one of these three men do you thing was a neighbor to the man who was attacked by robbers?"

The expert on the law answered, "The one who showed him mercy."

Jesus said to him, "Then go and do what he did."

Matthew 7:21 "Not all those who say that I am their Lord will enter the kingdom of heaven. The only people who will enter the kingdom of heaven are those who do what my Father in heaven wants."

God Knows Your Heart

Luke 16:14-15 The Pharisees, who loved money, were listening to all these things and made fun of Jesus. He said to them, "You make yourselves look good in front of people, but God knows what is really in your hearts. What is important to people is hateful in God's sight."

Romans 8:27 God can see what is in people's hearts. And he knows what is in the mind of the Spirit, because the Spirit speaks to God for his people in the way God wants.

God's Kingdom Within You

Luke 17:20-21 Some of the Pharisees asked Jesus, "When will the kingdom of God come?"

Jesus answered, "God's kingdom is coming, but not in a way that you will be able to see with your eyes. People will not say, 'Look, here it is!' or, 'There it is!' Because God's kingdom is within you."

Matthew 19:13-15 Then the people brought their little children to Jesus so he could put his hands on them and pray for them. His followers told them to stop, but Jesus said, "Let the little children come to me. Don't stop them, because the kingdom of heaven belongs to people who are like these children." After Jesus put his hands on the children, he left there.

Romans 14:17-18 In the Kingdom of God, eating and drinking are not important. The important things are living right with God, peace, and joy in the Holy Spirit. Anyone who serves Christ by living this way is pleasing God and will be accepted by other people.

Matthew 5:3 "Those people who know they have great spiritual needs are happy, because the kingdom of heaven belongs to them."

God's Kingdom Is Like...

Matthew 25:1-13 "At that time the kingdom of heaven will be like ten bridesmaids who took their lamps and went to wait for the bridegroom. Five of them were foolish and five were wise. The five foolish bridesmaids took their lamps, but they did not take more oil for the lamps to burn. The wise bridesmaids took their lamps and more oil in jars. Because the bridegroom was late, they became sleepy and went to sleep.

"At midnight someone cried out, 'The bridegroom is coming! Come and meet him!' Then all the bridesmaids woke up and got their lamps ready. But the foolish ones said to the wise, 'Give us some of your oil, because our lamps are going out.' The wise bridesmaids answered, 'No, the oil we have might not be enough for all of us. Go to the people who sell oil and buy some for yourselves.'

"So while the five foolish bridesmaids went to buy oil, the bridegroom came. The bridesmaids who were ready went in with the bridegroom to the wedding feast. Then the door was closed and locked.

"Later the others came back and said, 'Sir, sir, open the door to let us in.' But the bridegroom answered, 'I tell you the truth, I don't want to know you.'

"So always be ready, because you don't know the day or the hour the Son of Man will come."

Matthew 22:1-14 Jesus again used stories to teach the people. He said, "The kingdom of heaven is like a king who prepared a wedding feast for his son. The king invited some people to the feast. When the feast was ready, the king sent his servants to tell the people, but they refused to come.

"Then the king sent other servants, saying, 'Tell those who have been invited that my feast is ready. I have killed my best bulls and calves for the dinner, and everything is ready. Come to the wedding feast.'

"But the people refused to listen to the servants and left to do other things. One went to work in his field, and another went to his business. Some of the other people grabbed the servants, beat them, and killed them. The king was furious and sent his army to kill the murderers and burn their city.

"After that, the king said to his servants, 'The wedding feast is ready. I invited those people, but they were not worthy to come. So go to the street corners and invite everyone you find to come to my feast.' So the servants went into the streets and gathered all the people they could find, both good and bad. And the wedding hall was filled with guests.

"When the king came in to see the guests, he saw a man who was not dressed for a wedding. The king said, 'Friend, how were you allowed to come in here? You are not dressed for a wedding.' But the man said nothing. So the king told some servants, 'Tie this man's hands and feet. Throw him out into the darkness, where people will cry and grind their teeth with pain.'

"Yes, many people are invited, but only a few are chosen."

Matthew 13:24-30 Then Jesus told them another story: "The kingdom of heaven is like a man who planted good seed in his field. That night, when everyone was asleep, his enemy came and planted weeds among the wheat and then left. Later, the wheat sprouted and the heads of grain grew, but the weeds also grew. Then the man's servants came to him and said, 'You planted good seed in your field. Where did the weeds come from?' The man answered, 'An enemy planted weeds.' The servants asked, 'Do you want us to pull up the weeds?' The man answered, 'No, because when you pull up the weeds, you might also pull up the wheat. Let the weeds and the wheat grow together until the harvest time. At harvest time I will tell the workers, "First gather the weeds and tie them together to be burned. Then gather the wheat and bring it to my barn."'"

Matthew 13:31-35 (The story about Mustard Seed and Yeast) Then Jesus told another story: "The kingdom of heaven is like a mustard seed that a man planted in his field. That seed is the smallest of all seeds, but when it grows, it is one of the largest garden plants. It becomes big enough for the wild birds to come and build nests in its branches."

Then Jesus told another story: "The kingdom of heaven is like yeast that a woman took and hid in a large tub of flour until it made all the dough rise."

Jesus used stories to tell all these things to the people; he always used stories to teach them. This is as the prophet said:

"I will speak using stories;
I will tell things that have been secret since the
    world was made." (Psalm 78:2)

Matthew 13:44-46 "The kingdom of heaven is like a treasure hidden in a field. One day a man found the treasure, and then he hid it in the field again. He was so happy that he went and sold everything he owned to buy that field.

"Also, the kingdom of heaven is like a man looking for fine pearls. When he found a very valuable pearl, he went and sold everything he had and bought it."

Matthew 13:47-52 "Also, the kingdom of heaven is like a net that was put out into the lake and caught many different kinds of fish. When it was full, the fishermen pulled the net to the shore. They sat down and put all the good fish in baskets and threw away the bad fish. It will be this way at he end of the world. The angels will come and separate the evil people from the good people. The angels will throw the evil people into the blazing furnace, where people will cry and grind their teeth with pain."

Jesus asked his followers, "Do you understand all these things?"

They answered, "Yes, we understand."

Then Jesus said to them, "So every teacher of the law who has been taught about the kingdom of heaven is like the owner of a house. He brings out both new things and old things he has saved."

All People Are Guilty Of Sin

Romans 3:9-20 So are we Jews better than others? No! We have already said that Jews and those who are not Jews are all guilty of sin. As the Scriptures say:

> "There is no one who always does what is right,
> not even one.
> There is no one who understands.
> There is no one who looks to God for help.
> All have turned away.
> Together, everyone has become useless.
> There is no one who does anything good;
> there is not even one. (Psalm 14:1-3)
> "Their throats are like open graves;
> they use their tongues for telling lies." (Psalm 5:)
> "Their words are like snake poison." (Psalm 140:3)
> "Their mouths are full of cursing and hate." (Psalm 10:7)
> "They are always ready to kill people.
> Everywhere they go they cause ruin and misery.
> They don't know how to live in peace. (Isaiah 59:7-8)
> "They have no fear of God." (Psalm36:1)

We know that the law's commands are for those who have the law. This stops all excuses and brings the whole world under God's judgment, because no one can be made right with God by following the law. The law only shows us our sin.

Your Tongue Is Like A Rudder

James 3:1-12 My brothers and sisters, not many of you should become teachers, because you know that we who teach will be judged more strictly. We all make many mistakes. If people never said anything wrong, they would be perfect and able to control their entire selves, too. When we put bits into the mouths of horses to make them obey us, we can control their whole bodies. Also a ship is very big, and it is pushed by strong winds. But a very small rudder controls that big ship, making it go wherever the pilot wants. It is the same with the tongue. It is a small part of the body, but it brags about great things.

A big forest fire can be started with only a little flame. And the tongue is like a fire. It is a whole world of evil among the parts of our bodies. The tongue spreads its evil through the whole body. The tongue is set on fire by hell, and it starts a fire that influences all of life. People can tame every kind of wild animal, bird, reptile, and fish, and they have tamed them, but no one can tame the tongue. It is wild and evil and full of deadly poison. We use our tongues to praise our Lord and Father, but then we curse people, whom God made like himself. Praises and curses come from the same mouth! My brothers and sisters, this should not happen. Do good and bad water flow from the same spring? My brothers and sisters, can a fig tree make olives, or can a grapevine make figs? No! And a well full of salty water cannot give good water.

Matthew 12:33-37 "If you want good fruit, you must make the tree good. If your tree is not good, it will have bad fruit. A tree is known by the kind of fruit it produces. You snakes! You are evil people, so how can you say anything good? The mouth speaks the things that are in the heart. Good people have good things in their hearts, and so they say good things. But evil people have evil in their hearts, so they say evil things. And I tell you that on the Judgment Day people will be responsible for every careless thing they have said. The words you have said will be used to judge you. Some of your words will prove you right, but some of your words will prove you guilty."

The Word Became A Human

John 1:14 The Word became a human and lived among us. We saw his glory—the glory that belongs to the only Son of the Father—and he was full of grace and truth.

John 1:10-11 The Word was in the world, and the world was made by him, but the world did not know him. He came to the world that was his own, but his own people did not accept him.

John 1:1-5 In the beginning there was the Word. The Word was with God, and the Word was God. He was with God in the beginning. All things were made by him, and nothing was made without him. In him there was life, and that life was the light of all people. The Light shines in the darkness, and the darkness has not overpowered it.

The Lamb Of God—Son Of God Who Takes Away The Sin Of The World

John 1:29-34 The next day John saw Jesus coming toward him. John said, "Look, the Lamb of God, who takes away the sin of the world! This is the One I was talking about when I said, 'A man will come after me, but he is greater than I am, because he was living before me.' Even I did not know who he was, although I came baptizing with water so that the people of Israel would know who he is."

Then John said, "I saw the Spirit come down from heaven in the form of a dove and rest on him. Until then I did not know who the Christ was. But the God who sent me to baptize with water told me, 'You will see the Spirit come down and rest on a man; he is the One who will baptize with the Holy Spirit.' I have seen this happen, and I tell you the truth: This man is the Son of God."

John 3:16-21 "God loved the world so much that he gave his one and only Son so that whoever believes in him may not be lost, but have eternal life. God did not send his Son into the world to judge the world guilty, but to save the world through him. People who believe in God's Son are not judged guilty. Those who do not believe have already been judged guilty, because they have not believed in God's one and only Son. They are judged by this fact: The Light has come into the world, but they did not want light. They wanted darkness, because they were doing evil things. All who do evil hate the light and will not come to the light, because it will show all the evil things they do. But those who follow the true way come to the light, and it shows that the things they do were done through God."

2 Corinthians 5:21 Christ had no sin, but God made him become sin so that in Christ we could become right with God.

1 Thessalonians 1:10 And you wait for God's Son, whom God raised from the dead, to come from heaven. He is Jesus, who saves us from God's angry judgment that is sure to come.

God Brings People To Jesus

John 6:43 But Jesus answered, "Stop complaining to each other. The Father is the One who sent me. No one can come to me unless the Father draws him to me, and I will raise that person up on the last day."

John 6:65 Jesus said, "That is the reason I said, 'If the Father does not bring a person to me, that one cannot come.'"

1 Corinthians 1:24 But Christ is the power of God and the wisdom of God to those people God has called—Jews and Greeks.

2 Thessalonians 2:13-14 Brothers and sisters, who the Lord loves, God chose you from the beginning to be saved. So we must always thank God for you. You are saved by the Spirit that makes you holy and by your faith in the truth. God used the Good News that we preached to call you to be saved so you can share in the glory of our Lord Jesus Christ.

John 17:1-2 After Jesus said these things, he looked toward heaven and prayed, "Father, the time has come. Give glory to your Son so that the Son can give glory to you. You gave the Son power over all people so that the Son could give eternal life to all those you gave him."

John 17:6-9 "I showed what you are like to those you gave me from the world. They belonged to you, and you gave them to me, and they have obeyed your teaching. Now they know that everything you gave me comes from you. I gave them the teachings you gave me, and they accepted them. They knew that I truly came from you, and they believed that you sent me. I am praying for them. I am not praying for people in the world but for those you gave me, because they are yours."

Hebrews 9:15 For this reason Christ brings a new agreement from God to his people. Those who are called by God can now receive the blessings he has promised, blessings that will last forever. They can have those things because Christ died so that the people who lived under the first agreement could be set free from sin.

Romans 8:28-30 We know that in everything God works for the good of those who love him. They are the people he called, because that was his plan. God knew them before he made the world, and he decided that they would be like his Son so that Jesus would be the firstborn of many brothers. God planned for them to be like his Son; and those he planned to be like his Son, he also called; and those he called, he also made right with him; and those he made right, he also glorified.

Hebrews 2:13 He also says,
"I will trust in God." (Isaiah 8:17)
And he also says,
"I am here, and with me are the children God has given me." (Isaiah 8:18)

Matthew 15:13 Jesus answered, "Every plant that my Father in heaven has not planted himself will be pulled up by the roots."

God Chooses Who He Wants, Not Because Of Anything We Do

Romans 9:9-18 God's promise to Abraham was this: "At the right time I will return, and Sarah will have a son." And that is not all. Rebekah's sons had the same father, our father Isaac. But before the two boys were born, God told Rebekah, "The older will serve the younger." This was before the boys had done anything good or bad. God said this so that the one chosen would be chosen because of God's own plan. He was chosen because he was the one God wanted to call, not because of anything he did. As the Scripture says, "I loved Jacob, but I hated Esau."

So what should we say about this? Is God unfair? In no way. God said to Moses, "I will show kindness to anyone to whom I want to show kindness, and I will show mercy to anyone to whom I want to show mercy." So God will choose the one to whom he decides to show mercy; his choice does not depend on what people want or try to do. The Scripture says to the king of Egypt: "I made you king for this reason: to show my power in you so that my name will be talked about in all the earth." So God shows mercy where he wants to show mercy, and he makes stubborn the people he wants to make stubborn.

Romans 11:1-7 So I ask: Did God throw out his people? No! I myself am an Israelite from the family of Abraham, from the tribe of Benjamin. God chose the Israelites to be his people before they were born, and he has not thrown his people out. Surely you know what the Scripture says about Elijah, how he prayed to God against the people of Israel. "Lord," he said, "they have killed your prophets, and they have destroyed your altars. I am the only prophet left, and now they are tying to kill me, too." But what answer did God give Elijah? He said, "But I have left seven thousand people in Israel who have never bowed down before Baal." It is the same now. There are a few people that God has chosen by his grace. And if he chose them by grace, it is not for the things they have done. If they could be made God's people by what they did, God's gift of grace would not really be a gift.

So this is what has happened: Although the Israelites tried to be right with God, they did not succeed, but the ones God chose did become right with him. The others were made stubborn and refused to listen to God.

Romans 8:28-30 We know that in everything God works for the good of those who love him. They are the people he called, because that was his plan. God knew them before he made the world, and he decided that they would be like his Son so that Jesus would be the firstborn of many brothers. God planned for them to be like his Son; and those he planned to be like his Son, he also called; and those he called, he also made right with him; and those he made right, he also glorified.

Be Sure You Are Chosen By God

2 Peter 1:10-11 My brothers and sisters, try hard to be certain that you really are called and chosen by God. If you do all these things, you will never fall. And you will be given a very great welcome into the eternal kingdom of our Lord and Savior Jesus Christ.

2 Peter 1:5-9 Because you have these blessings, do your best to add these things to your lives: to your faith, add goodness; and to your goodness, add knowledge; and to your knowledge, add self-control; and to your self-control, add patience; and to your patience, add service for God; and to your service for God, add kindness for your brothers and sisters in Christ; and to this kindness, add love. If all these things are in you and are growing, they will help you to be useful and productive in your knowledge of our Lord Jesus Christ. But anyone who does not have these things cannot see clearly. He is blind and has forgotten that he was made clean from his past sins.

1 John 2:3-6 We can be sure that we know God if we obey his commands. Anyone who says, "I know God," but does not obey God's commands is a liar, and the truth is not in that person. But if someone obeys God's teaching, then in that person God's love has truly reached its goal. This is how we can be sure we are living in God: Whoever says that he lives in God must live as Jesus lived.

1 John 3:19-21 This is the way we know that we belong to the way of truth. When our hearts make us feel guilty, we can still have peace before God. God is greater than our hearts, and he knows everything. My dear friends, if our hearts do not make us feel guilty, we can come without fear into God's presence.

1 John 3:9-10 Those who are God's children do not continue sinning, because the new life from God remains in them. They are not able to go on sinning, because they have become children of God. So we can see who God's children are and who the devil's children are: Those who do not do what is right are not God's children, and those who do not love their brothers and sisters are not God's children.

Jesus Heals Spiritual Blindness

John 9:35-41 When Jesus heard that they had thrown him out, Jesus found him and said, "Do you believe in the Son of Man?"

He asked, "Who is the Son of Man, sir, so that I can believe in him?"

Jesus said to him, "You have seen him. The Son of Man is the one talking with you."

He said, "Lord, I believe!" Then the man worshiped Jesus.

Jesus said, "I came into this world so that the world could be judged. I came so that the blind would see and so that those who see will become blind."

Some of the Pharisees who were nearby heard Jesus say this and asked, "Are you saying we are blind, too?"

Jesus said, "If you were blind, you would not be guilty of sin. But since you keep saying you see, your guilt remains."

Why Didn't Jesus Show Himself To The World?

I've heard several Jewish leaders ask this same question: "After Jesus' resurrection, why didn't he show himself to the whole world?" One Jewish scholar, speaking hypothetically said, "If only there had been a camera to take a picture of the resurrected Jesus then we would have the proof."

John 14:22-31 Then Judas (not Judas Iscariot) said, "But, Lord, why do you plan to show yourself to us and not to the rest of the world?"

Jesus answered, "If people love me, they will obey my teaching. My Father will love them, and we will come to them and make our home with them. Those who do not love me do not obey my teaching. This teaching that you hear is not really mine; it is from my Father, who sent me.

"I have told you all these things while I am with you. But the Helper will teach you everything and will cause you to remember all that I told you. This Helper is the Holy Spirit whom the Father will send in my name.

"I leave you peace; my peace I give you. I do not give it to you as the world does. So don't let your hearts be troubled or afraid. You heard me say to you, 'I am going, but I am coming back to you.' If you loved me, you should be happy that I am going back to the Father, because he is greater than I am. I have told you this now, before it happens, so that when it happens, you will believe. I will not talk with you much longer, because the ruler of this world is coming. He has no power over me, but the world must know that I love the Father, so I do exactly what the Father told me to do.

"Come now, let us go."

John 16:8-11 "When the Helper comes, he will prove to the people of the world the truth about sin, about being right with God, and about judgment. He will prove to them that sin is not believing in me. He will prove to them that being right with God comes from my going to the Father and not being seen anymore. And the Helper will prove to them that judgment happened when the ruler of this world was judged."

John 20:24-29 Thomas (called Didymus), who was one of the twelve, was not with them when Jesus came. The other followers kept telling Thomas, "We saw the Lord."

But Thomas said, "I will not believe it until I see the nail marks in his hands and put my finger where the nails were and put my hand into his side."

A week later the followers were in the house again, and Thomas was with them. The doors were locked, but Jesus came in and stood right in the middle of them. He said, "Peace be with you." Then he said to Thomas, "Put your finger here, and look at my hands. Put your hand here in my side. Stop being an unbeliever and believe."

Thomas said to him, "My Lord and my God!"

Then Jesus told him, "You believe because you see me. Those who believe without seeing me will be truly happy."

1 Corinthians 15:3-8 I passed on to you what I received, of which this was most important: that Christ died for out sins, as the Scriptures say; that he was buried and was raised to life on the third day as the Scriptures say; and that he was seen by Peter and then by the twelve apostles. After that, Jesus was seen by more than five hundred of the believers at the same time. Most of them are still living today, but some have died. Then he was seen by James and later by all the apostles. Last of all he was seen by me—as by a person not born at the normal time.

Sin Is Not Believing In Christ: There Is No Sin In Christ

John 16:8-11 When the Helper comes, he will prove to the people of the world the truth about sin, about being right with God, and about judgment. He will prove to them that sin is not believing in me. He will prove to them that being right with God comes from my going to the Father and not being seen anymore. And the Helper will prove to them that judgment happened when the ruler of this world was judged.

1 John 3:4-10 The person who sins breaks God's law. Yes, sin is living against God's law. You know that Christ came to take away sins and that there is no sin in Christ. So anyone who lives in Christ does not go on sinning. Anyone who goes on sinning has never really understood Christ and has never known him.

Dear children, do not let anyone lead you the wrong way. Christ is all that is right. So to be like Christ a person must do what is right. The devil has been sinning since the beginning, so anyone who continues to sin belongs to the devil. The Son of God came for this purpose: to destroy the devil's work.

Those who are God's children do not continue sinning, because the new life from God remains in them. They are not able to go on sinning, because they have become children of God. So we can see who God's children are and who the devil's children are: Those who do not do what is right are not God's children, and those who do not love their brothers and sisters are not God's children.

Jesus Is Truth

John 14:6-7 Jesus answered, "I am the way, and the truth, and the life. The only way to the Father is through me. If you really knew me, you would know my Father, too. But now you do know him, and you have seen him."

John 18:37-38 Pilate said, "So you are a king!"

Jesus answered, "You are the one saying I am a king. This is why I was born and came into the world: to tell people the truth. And everyone who belongs to the truth listens to me."

Pilate said, "What is truth?" After he said this, he went out to the Jews again and said to them, "I find nothing against this man."

John 1:14 The Word became a human and lived among us. We saw his glory—the glory that belongs to the only Son of the Father—and he was full of grace and truth.

John 1:16-17 Because he was full of grace and truth, from him we all received one gift after another. The law was given through Moses, but grace and truth came through Jesus Christ.

2 Thessalonians 2:9-12 The Man of Evil will come by the power of Satan. He will have great power, and he will do many different false miracles, signs, and wonders. He will use every kind of evil to trick those who are lost. They will die, because they refused to love the truth. (If they loved the truth, they would be saved.) For this reason God sends them something powerful that leads them away from the truth so they will believe a lie. So all those will be judged guilty who did not believe the truth, but enjoyed doing evil.

1 John 5:10 Anyone who believes in the Son of God has the truth that God told us. Anyone who does not believe makes God a liar, because that person does not believe what God told us about his Son.

1 John 2:20-21 You have the gift that the Holy One gave you, so you all know the truth. I do not write to you because you do not know the truth but because you do know the truth. And you know that no lie comes from the truth.

Anyone Who Doesn't Believe In Jesus—
Is A Liar—Makes God A Liar

1 John 5:10-12 Anyone who believes in the Son of God has the truth that God told us. Anyone who does not believe makes God a liar, because that person does not believe what God told us about his Son. This is what God told us: God has given us eternal life, and this life is in his Son. Whoever has the Son has life, but whoever does not have the Son of God does not have life.

1 John 2:22-23 Who is the liar? It is the person who does not accept Jesus as the Christ. This is the enemy of Christ: the person who does not accept the Father and his Son. Whoever does not accept the Son does not have the Father. But whoever confesses the Son has the Father, too.

Did Paul Kill Christians?

Acts 9:13-14 But Ananias answered, "Lord, many people have told me about this man and the terrible things he did to your holy people in Jerusalem. Now he has come here to Damascus, and the leading priests have given him the power to arrest everyone who worships you."

Acts 9:1-2 In Jerusalem Saul was still threatening the followers of the Lord by saying he would kill them. So he went to the high priest and asked him to write letters to the synagogues in the city of Damascus. Then if Saul found any follower's of Christ's Way, men or women, he would arrest them and bring them back to Jerusalem.

Acts 22:4-5 "I persecuted the people who followed the Way of Jesus, and some of them were even killed. I arrested men and women and put them in jail. The high priest and the whole council of older Jewish leaders can tell you this is true. They gave me letters to the Jewish brothers in Damascus. So I was going there to arrest these people and bring them back to Jerusalem to be punished."

Acts 26:9-11 "I, too, thought I ought to do many things against Jesus from Nazareth. And that is what I did in Jerusalem. The leading priests gave me the power to put many of God's people in jail, and when they were being killed, I agreed it was a good thing. In every synagogue, I often punished them and tried to make them speak against Jesus. I was so angry against them I even went to other cities to find them and punish them."

Jesus Appears To Saul: Paul's Conversion

Acts 9:3-9 So Saul headed toward Damascus. As he came near the city, a bright light from heaven suddenly flashed around him. Saul fell to the ground and heard a voice saying to him, "Saul, Saul! Why are you persecuting me?"

Saul said, "Who are you, Lord?"

The voice answered, "I am Jesus, whom you are persecuting. Get up now and go into the city. Someone there will tell you what you must do."

The people traveling with Saul stood there but said nothing. They heard the voice, but they saw no one. Saul got up from the ground and opened his eyes, but he could not see. So those with Saul took his hand and led him into Damascus. For three days Saul could not see and did not eat or drink.

Acts 23:11 The next night the Lord came and stood by Paul. He said, "Be brave! You have told people in Jerusalem about me. You must do the same in Rome."

Paul's Most Important Thing Is To Tell About The Good News

Acts 20:24 "I don't care about my own life. The most important thing is that I complete my mission, the work that the Lord Jesus gave me—to tell people the Good News about God's grace."

Romans 1:1-7 From Paul, a servant of Christ Jesus. God called me to be an apostle and chose me to tell the Good News.

God promised this Good News long ago through his prophets, as it is written in the Holy Scriptures. The Good News is about God's Son, Jesus Christ our Lord. As a man, he was born from the family of David. But through the Spirit of holiness he was appointed to be God's Son with great power by rising from the dead. Through Christ, God gave me the special work of an apostle, which was to lead people of all nations to believe and obey. I do this work for him. And you who are in Rome are also called to belong to Jesus Christ.

To all of you in Rome whom God loves and has called to be his holy people: Grace and peace to you from God our Father and the Lord Jesus Christ.

1 Timothy 2:5-7 There is one God and one way human beings can reach God. That way is through Christ Jesus, who is himself human. He gave himself as a payment to free all people. He is proof that came at the right time. That is why I was chosen to tell the Good News and to be an apostle. (I am telling the truth; I am not lying.) I was chosen to teach those who are not Jews to believe and to know the truth.

Ephesians 3:7-11 By God's special gift of grace given to me through his power, I became a servant to tell the Good News. I am the least important of all God's people, but God gave me this gift—to tell those who are not Jews the Good News about the riches of Christ, which are too great to understand fully. And God gave me the work of telling all people about the plan for his secret, which has been hidden in him since the beginning of time. He is the One who created everything. His purpose was that through the church all the rulers and powers in the heavenly world will now know God's wisdom, which has so many forms. This agrees with the purpose God had since the beginning of time, and he carried out his plan through Christ Jesus our Lord.

Wild Olive Tree And Non-Jewish People:
Keep Believing & Following God Or Be Cut Off

Romans 11:1-32 So I ask: Did God throw out his people? No! I myself am an Israelite from the family of Abraham, from the tribe of Benjamin. God chose the Israelites to be his people before they were born, and he has not thrown his people out. Surely you know what the Scripture says about Elijah, how he prayed to God against the people of Israel. "Lord," he said, "they have killed your prophets, and they have destroyed your altars. I am the only prophet left, and now they are trying to kill me, too." But what answer did God give Elijah? He said, "But I have left seven thousand people in Israel who have never bowed down before Baal." It is the same now. There are a few people that God has chosen by his grace. And if he chose them by grace, it is not for the things they have done. If they could be made God's people by what they did, God's gift of grace would not really be a gift.

So this is what has happened: Although the Israelites tried to be right with God, they did not succeed, but the ones God chose did become right with him. The others were made stubborn and refused to listen to God. As it is written in the Scriptures:

"God gave the people a dull mind so they could not understand." (Isaiah 29:10)
"He closed their eyes so they could not see
and their ears so they could not hear.
This continues until today." (Deuteronomy 29:4)

And David says:

"Let their own feasts trap them and cause their ruin;
let their feasts cause them to stumble and be paid back.
Let their eyes be closed so they cannot see
and their backs be forever weak from troubles." (Psalm 69:22-23)

So I ask: When the Jews fell, did that fall destroy them? No! But their mistake brought salvation to those who are not Jews, in order to make the Jews jealous. The Jews' mistake brought rich blessings for the world, and the Jews' loss brought rich blessings for the non-Jewish people. So surely the world will receive much richer blessings when enough Jews become the kind of people God wants.

Now I am speaking to you who are not Jews. I am an apostle to those who are not Jews, and since I have that work, I will make the most of it. I hope I can make my own people jealous and, in that way, help some of them to be saved. When God turned away from the Jews, he became friends with other people in the world. So when God accepts the Jews, surely that will bring them life after death.

If the first piece of bread is offered to God, then the whole loaf is made holy. If the roots of a tree are holy, then the tree's branches are holy too.

It is as if some of the branches from an olive tree have been broken off. You non-Jewish people are like the branch of a wild olive tree that has been joined to the first tree. You now share the strength and life of the first tree, the Jews. So do not brag about those branches that were broken off. If you brag, remember that you do not support the root, but the root supports you. You will say, "Branches were broken off so that I could be joined to their tree." That is true. But those branches were broken off because they did not believe, and you continue to be part of the tree only because you believe. Do not be proud, but be afraid. **If God did not let the natural branches of that tree stay, then he will not let you stay if you don't believe**.

So you see that God is kind and also very strict. He punishes those who stop following him. But God is kind to you, if you continue following in his kindness. If you do not, you will be cut off from the tree. And if the Jews will believe in God again, he will accept them back. God is able to put them back where they were. It is not natural for a wild branch to be part of a good tree. And you who are not Jews are like a branch cut from a wild olive tree and joined to a good olive tree. But since those Jews are like a branch that grew from the good tree, surely they can be joined to their own tree again.

I want you to understand this secret, brothers and sisters, so you will understand that you do not know everything: **Part of Israel has been made stubborn, but that will change when many who are not Jews have come to God. And that is how all Israel will be saved**. It is written in the Scriptures:

> "The Savior will come from Jerusalem;
> he will take away all evil from the family of Jacob."
> And I will make this agreement with those people
> when I take away their sins." (Isaiah 59:20-21; 27:9)

The Jews refuse to accept the Good News, so they are God's enemies. This has happened to help you who are not Jews. But the Jews are still God's chosen people, and he loves them very much because of the promises he made to their ancestors. God never changes his mind about the people he calls and the things he gives them. At one time you refused to obey God. But now you have received mercy, because those people refused to obey. And now the Jews refuse to obey, because God showed mercy to you. But this happened so that they also can receive mercy from him. God has given all people over to their stubborn ways so that he can show mercy to all.

Do Not Judge Others

Romans 2:1-3 If you think you can judge others, you are wrong. When you judge them, you are really judging yourself guilty, because you do the same things they do. God judges those who do wrong things, and we know that his judging is right. You judge those who do wrong, but you do wrong yourselves. Do you think you will be able to escape the judgment of God?

Romans 14:9-13 The reason Christ died and rose from the dead to live again was so he would be Lord over both the dead and the living. So why do you judge your brothers or sisters in Christ? And why do you think you are better than they are? We will all stand before God to be judged, because it is written in the Scriptures:

> "'As surely as I live,' says the Lord,
> 'Everyone will bow before me;
> everyone will say that I am God.'" (Isaiah 45:23)

So each of us will have to answer to God.

For that reason we should stop judging each other. We must make up our minds not to do anything that will make another Christian sin.

1 Corinthians 5:12-13 It is not my business to judge those who are not part of the church. God will judge them. But you must judge the people who are part of the church. The Scripture says, "You must get rid of the evil person among you."

James 4:11-12 Brothers and sisters, do not tell evil lies about each other. If you speak against your fellow believers or judge them, you are judging and speaking against the law they follow. And when you are judging the law, you are no longer a follower of the law. You have become a judge. God is the only Lawmaker and Judge. He is the only One who can save and destroy. So it is not right for you to judge your neighbor.

Matthew 13:24-30 (The story about wheat and weeds) Then Jesus told them another story: "The kingdom of heaven is like a man who planted good seed in his field. That night, when everyone was asleep, his enemy came and planted weeds among the wheat and then left. Later, the wheat sprouted and the heads of grain grew, but the weeds also grew. Then the man's servants came to him and said, 'You planted good seed in your field. Where did the weeds come from?' The man answered, 'An enemy planted weeds.' The servants asked, 'Do you want us to pull up the weeds?' The man answered, 'No, because when you pull up the weeds, you might also pull up the wheat. Let the weeds and the wheat grow together until the harvest time. At harvest time I will tell the workers, "First gather the weeds and tie them together to be burned. Then gather the wheat and bring it to my barn.""

John 8:1-11 Jesus went to the Mount of Olives. But early in the morning he went back to the Temple, and all the people came to him, and he sat and taught them. The teachers of the law and the Pharisees brought a woman who had been caught in adultery. They forced her to stand before the people. They said to Jesus, "Teacher, this woman was caught having sexual relations with a man who is not her husband. The law of Moses commands that we stone to death every woman who does this. What do you say we should do?" They were asking this to trick Jesus so that they could have some charge against him.

But Jesus bent over and started writing on the ground with his finger. When they continued to ask Jesus their question, he raised up and said, "Anyone here who has never sinned can throw the first stone at her." Then Jesus bent over again and wrote on the ground.

Those who heard Jesus began to leave one by one, first the older men and then the others. Jesus was left there alone with the woman standing before him. Jesus raised up again and asked her, "Woman, where are they? Has no one judged you guilty?"

She answered, "No one, sir."

Then Jesus said, "I also don't judge you guilty. You may go now, but don't sin anymore."

John 12:47-48 "Anyone who hears my words and does not obey them, I do not judge, because I did not come to judge the world, but to save the world. There is a judge for those who refuse to believe in me and do not accept my words. The word I have taught will be their judge on the last day."

Luke 6:37-42 "Don't judge other people, and you will not be judged. Don't accuse others of being guilty, and you will not be accused of being guilty. Forgive, and you will be forgiven. Give, and you will receive. You will be given much. Pressed down, shaken together, and running over, it will spill into your lap. The way you give to others is the way God will give to you."

Jesus told them this story: "Can a blind person lead another blind person? No! Both of them will fall into a ditch. A student is not better than the teacher, but the student who has been fully trained will be like the teacher.

"Why do you notice the little piece of dust in your friend's eye, but you don't notice the big piece of wood in your own eye? How can you say to your friend, 'Friend, let me take that little piece of dust out of your eye' when you cannot see that big piece of wood in your own eye! You hypocrite! First, take the wood out of your own eye. Then you will see clearly to take the dust out of your friend's eye."

Man Without Knowledge Of God Will Be Sinful

Romans 1:28-32 People did not think it was important to have a true knowledge of God. So God left them and allowed them to have their own worthless thinking and to do things they should not do. They are filled with every kind of sin, evil, selfishness, and hatred. They are full of jealousy, murder, fighting, lying, and thinking the worst about each other. They gossip and say evil things about each other. They hate God. They are rude and conceited and brag about themselves. They invent ways of doing evil. They do not obey their parents. They are foolish, they do not keep their promises, and they show no kindness or mercy to others. They know God's law says that those who live like this should die. But they themselves not only continue to do these evil things, they applaud others who do them.

If There Is No Punishment, There Is No Judgment

Romans 3:5-8 When we do wrong, that shows more clearly that God is right. So can we say that God is wrong to punish us? (I am talking as people might talk.) No! If God could not punish us, he could not judge the world.

A person might say, "When I lie, it really gives him glory, because my lie shows God's truth. So why am I judged a sinner?" It would be the same to say, "We should do evil so that good will come." Some people find fault with us and say we teach this, but they are wrong and deserve the punishment they will receive.

Adam And Christ Compared

Romans 5:12-21 Sin came into the world because of what one man did, and with sin came death. This is why everyone must die—because everyone sinned. Sin was in the world before the law of Moses, but sin is not counted against us as breaking a command when there is no law. But from the time of Adam to the time of Moses, everyone had to die, even those who had not sinned by breaking a command, as Adam had.

Adam was like the One who was coming in the future. But God's free gift is not like Adam's sin. Many people died because of the sin of that one man. But the grace from God was much greater; many people received God's gift of life by the grace of the one man, Jesus Christ. After Adam sinned once, he was judged guilty. But the gift of God is different. God's free gift came after many sins, and it makes people right with God. One man sinned, and so death ruled all people because of that one man. But now those people who accept God's full grace and the great gift of being made right with him will surely have true life and rule through the one man, Jesus Christ.

So as one sin of Adam brought the punishment of death to all people, one good act that Christ did makes all people right with God. And that brings true life for all. One man disobeyed God, and many became sinners. In the same way, one man obeyed God, and many will be made right. The law came to make sin worse. But when sin grew worse, God's grace increased. Sin once used death to rule us, but God gave people more of his grace so that grace could rule by making people right with him. And this brings life forever through Jesus Christ our Lord.

1 Corinthians 15:21-22 Death has come because of what one man did, but the rising from death also comes because of one man. In Adam all of us die. In the same way, in Christ all of us will be made alive again.

Your Body Is A Temple For The Holy Spirit:
Run From Sexual Sin

1 Corinthians 6:18-20 So run away from sexual sin. Every other sin people do is outside their bodies, but hose who sin sexually sin against their own bodies. You should know that your body is a temple for the Holy Spirit who is in you. You have received the Holy Spirit from God. So you do not belong to yourselves, because you were bought by God for a price. So honor God with your bodies.

Stephen And Paul Tell The History From Abraham To King David

Acts 7:1-52 The high priest said to Stephen, "Are these things true?"

Stephen answered, "Brothers and fathers, listen to me. Our glorious God appeared to Abraham, our ancestor, in Mesopotamia before he lived in Haran....

Acts 13:16-41 Paul stood up, raised his hand, and said, "You Israelites and you who worship God, please listen!...

Nothing In The Whole World Can
Separate Us From TheLove Of God In Jesus

Romans 8:33-39 Who can accuse the people God has chosen? No one, because God is the One who makes them right. Who can say God's people are guilty? No one, because Christ Jesus died, but he was also raised from the dead, and now he is on God's right side, begging God for us. Can anything separate us from the love Christ has for us? Can troubles or problems or sufferings or hunger or nakedness or danger or violent death? As it is written in the Scriptures:

> "For you we are in danger of death all the time.
> People think we are worth no more than sheep to
> be killed." (Psalm 44:22)

But in all things we have full victory through God who showed his love for us. Yes, I am sure that neither death, nor life, nor angels, nor ruling spirits, nothing now, nothing in the future, no powers, nothing above us, nothing below us, nor anything else in the whole world will ever be able to separate us from the love of God that is in Christ Jesus our Lord.

Our Part As Christians — As Part Of The Body

Romans 12:4-13 Each one of us has a body with many parts, and these parts all have different uses. In the same way, we are many, but in Christ we are all one body. Each one is a part of that body, and each part belongs to all the other parts. We all have different gifts, each of which came because of the grace God gave us. The person who has the gift of prophecy should use that gift in agreement with faith. Anyone who has the gift of serving should serve. Anyone who has the gift of teaching should teach. Whoever has the gift of encouraging others should encourage. Whoever has the gift of giving to others should give freely. Anyone who has the gift of being a leader should try hard when he leads. Whoever has the gift of showing mercy to others should do so with joy.

Your love must be real. Hate what is evil, and hold on to what is good. Love each other like brothers and sisters. Give each other more honor than you want for yourselves. Do not be lazy but work hard, serving the Lord with all your heart. Be joyful because you have hope. Be patient when trouble comes, and pray at all times. Share with God's people who need help. Bring strangers in need into your homes.

1 Corinthians 12:14-31 The human body has many parts. The foot might say, "Because I am not a hand, I am not part of the body." But saying this would not stop the foot from being a part of the body. The ear might say, "Because I am not an eye, I am not part of the body." But saying this would not stop the ear from being a part of the body. If the whole body were an eye, it would not be able to hear. If the whole body were an ear, it would not be able to smell. If each part of the body were the same part, there would be no body. But truly God put all the parts, each one of them, in the body as he wanted them. So then there are many parts, but only one body.

The eye cannot say to the hand, "I don't need you!" And the head cannot say to the foot, "I don't need you!" No! Those parts of the body that seem to be the weaker are really necessary. And the parts of the body we think are less deserving are the parts to which we give the most honor. We give special respect to the parts we want to hide. The more respectable parts of our body need no special care. But God put the body together and gave more honor to the parts that need it so our body would not be divided. God wanted the different parts to care the same for each other. If one part of the body suffers, all the other parts suffer with it. Or if one part of our body is honored, all the other parts share its honor.

Together you are the body of Christ, and each one of you is a part of that body. In the church God has given a place first to apostles, second to prophets, and third to teachers. Then God has given a place to those who do miracles, those who have gifts of healing, those who can help others, those who are able to govern, and those who can speak in different languages. Not all are apostles. Not all are prophets. Not all are teachers. Not all do miracles. Not all have gifts of healing. Not all speak in different languages. Not all interpret those languages. But you should truly want to have the greater gifts.

Romans 14:19 So let us try to do what makes peace and helps one another.

Ephesians 4:11-13 And Christ gave gifts to people—he made some to be apostles, some to be prophets, some to go and tell the Good News, and some to have the work of caring for and teaching God's people. Christ gave those gifts to prepare God's holy people for the work of serving, to make the body of Christ stronger. This work must continue until we are all joined together in the same faith and in the same knowledge of the Son of God. We must become like a mature person, growing until we become like Christ and have his perfection.

Brag Only About The Lord

1 Corinthians 1:27-31 But God chose the foolish things of the world to shame the wise, and he chose the weak things of the world to shame the strong. He chose what the world thinks is unimportant and what the world looks down on and thinks is nothing in order to destroy what the world thinks is important. God did this so that no one can brag in his presence. Because of God you are in Christ Jesus, who has become for us wisdom from God. In Christ we are put right with God, and have been made holy, and have been set free from sin. So, as the Scripture says, "If someone wants to brag, he should brag only about the Lord."

1 Corinthians 4:6-7 Brothers and sisters, I have used Apollos and myself as examples so you could learn through us the meaning of the saying, "Follow only what is written in the Scriptures." Then you will not be more proud of one person than another. Who says you are better than others? What do you have that was not given to you? And if it was given to you, why do you brag as if you did not receive it as a gift?

Romans 3:27-28 So do we have a reason to brag about ourselves? No! And why not? It is the way of faith that stops all bragging, not the way of trying to obey the law. A person is made right with God through faith, not through obeying the law.

The Spirit In Us Knows Our Thoughts: We Receive The Spirit From God: Live By Following The Spirit

1 Corinthians 2:10-16 But God has shown us these things through the Spirit. The Spirit searches out all things, even the deep secrets of God. Who knows the thoughts that another person has? Only a person's spirit that lives within him knows his thoughts. It is the same with God. No one knows the thoughts of God except the Spirit of God. Now we did not receive the spirit of the world, but we received the Spirit that is from God so that we can know all that God has given us. And we speak about these things, not with words taught us by human wisdom but with words taught us by the Spirit. And so we explain spiritual truths to spiritual people. A person who does not have the Spirit does not accept the truths that come from the Spirit of God. That person thinks they are foolish and cannot understand them, because they can only be judged to be true by the Spirit. The spiritual person is able to judge all things, but no one can judge him. The Scripture says:

> "Who has known the mind of the Lord?
> Who has been able to teach him?" (Isaiah 40:13)
> But we have the mind of Christ.

1 Corinthians 3:3-4 You are still not spiritual, because there is jealousy and quarreling among you, and this shows that you are not spiritual. You are acting like people of the world. One of you says, "I belong to Paul," and another says, "I belong to Apollos." When you say things like this, you are acting like people of the world.

2 Corinthians 3:1-3 Are we starting to brag about ourselves again? Do we need letters of introduction to you or from you, like some other people? You yourselves are our letter, written on our hearts, known and read by everyone. You show that you are a letter from Christ sent through us. This letter is not written with ink but with the Spirit of the living God. **It is not written on stone tablets but on human hearts**.

2 Corinthians 5:5 This is what God made us for, and he has given us the Spirit to be a guarantee for this new life.

1 Peter 3:18 Christ himself suffered for sins once. He was not guilty, but he suffered for those who are guilty to bring you to God. His body was killed, but he was made alive in the spirit.

2 Thessalonians 2:13 Brothers and sisters, whom the Lord loves, God chose you from the beginning to be saved. So we must always thank God for you. You are saved by the Spirit that makes you holy and by your faith in the truth.

1 Corinthians 6:17 But the one who joins with the Lord is one spirit with the Lord.

1 John 3:24 The people who obey God's commands live in God, and God lives in them. We know that God lives in us because of the Spirit God gave us.

1 John 4:1-6 My dear friends, many false prophets have gone out into the world. So do not believe every spirit, but test the spirits to see if they are from God. This is how you can know God's Spirit: Every spirit who confesses that Jesus Christ came to earth as a human is from God. And every spirit who refuses to say this about Jesus is not from God. It is the spirit of the enemy of Christ, which you have heard is coming, and now he is already in the world.

My dear children, you belong to God and have defeated them; because God's Spirit, who is in you, is greater than the devil, who is in the world. And they belong to the world, so what they say is from the world, and the world listens to them. But we belong to God, and those who know God listen to us. But those who are not from God do not listen to us. This is how we know the Spirit that is true and the spirit that is false.

1 John 4:13 We know that we live in God and he lives in us, because he gave us his Spirit.

Romans 8:1-27 So now, those who are in Christ Jesus are not judged guilty. Through Christ Jesus the law of the Spirit that brings life made me free from the law that brings sin and death. The law was without power, because the law was made weak by our sinful selves. But God did what the law could not do. He sent his own Son to earth with the same human life that others use for sin. By sending his Son to be an offering to pay for sin, God used a human life to destroy sin. He did this so that we could be the kind of people the law correctly wants us to be. Now we do not live following our sinful selves, but we live following the Spirit.

Those who live following their sinful selves think only about things that their sinful selves want. But those who live following the Spirit are thinking about the things the Spirit wants them to do. If people's thinking is controlled by the sinful self, there is death. But if their thinking is controlled by the Spirit, there is life and peace. When people's thinking is controlled by the sinful self, they are against God, because they refuse to obey God's law and really are not even able to obey God's law. Those people who are ruled by their sinful selves cannot please God.

But you are not ruled by your sinful selves. You are ruled by the Spirit, if that Spirit of God really lives in you. But the person who does not have the Spirit of Christ does not belong to Christ. Your body will always be dead because of sin. But if Christ is in you, then the Spirit gives you life, because Christ made you right with God. God raised Jesus from the dead, and if God's Spirit is living in you, he will also give life to your bodies that die. God is the One who raised Christ from the dead, and he will give life through his Spirit that lives in you.

So, my brothers and sisters, we must not be ruled by our sinful selves or live the way our sinful selves want. If you use your lives to do the wrong things your sinful selves want, you will die spiritually. But if you use the Spirit's help to stop doing the wrong things you do with your body, you will have true life.

The true children of God are those who let God's Spirit lead them. The Spirit we received does not make us slaves again to fear; it makes us children of God. With that Spirit we cry out, "Father." And the Spirit himself joins with our spirits to say we are God's children. If we are God's children, we will receive blessings from God together with Christ. But we must suffer as Christ suffered so that we will have glory as Christ has glory.

The sufferings we have now are nothing compared to the great glory that will be shown to us. Everything God made is waiting with excitement for God to show his children's glory completely. Everything God made was changed to become useless, not by its own wish but because God wanted it and because all along there was this hope: that everything God made would be set free from ruin to have the freedom and glory that belong to God's children.

We know that everything God made has been waiting until now in pain, like a woman ready to give birth. Not only the world, but we also have been waiting with pain inside us. We have the Spirit as the first part of God's promise. So we are waiting for God to finish making us his own children, which means our bodies will be made free. We were saved, and we have this hope. If we see what we are waiting for, that is not really hope. People do not hope for something they already have. But we are hoping for something we do not have yet, and we are waiting for it patiently.

Also, the Spirit helps us with our weakness. We do not know how to pray as we should. But the Spirit himself speaks to God for us, even begs God for us with deep feelings that words cannot explain. God can see what is in people's hearts. And he knows what is in the mind of the Spirit, because the Spirit speaks to God for his people in the way God wants.

Galatians 5:16-26 So I tell you: Live by following the Spirit. Then you will not do what your sinful selves want. Our sinful selves want what is against the Spirit, and the Spirit wants what is against our sinful selves. The two are against each other, so you cannot do just what you please. But if the Spirit is leading you, you are not under the law.

The wrong things the sinful self does are clear: being sexually unfaithful, not being pure, taking part in sexual sins, worshiping gods, doing witchcraft, hating, making trouble, being jealous, being angry, being selfish, making people angry with each other, causing divisions among people, feeling envy, being drunk, having wild and wasteful parties, and doing other things like these. I warn you now as I warned you before: Those who do these things will not inherit God's kingdom. But the Spirit produces the fruit of love, joy, peace, patience, kindness, goodness, faithfulness, gentleness, self-control. There is no law that says these things are wrong. Those who belong to Christ Jesus have crucified their own sinful selves. They have given up their old selfish feelings and the evil things they wanted to do. We get our new life from the Spirit, so we should follow the Spirit. We must not be proud or make trouble with each other or be jealous of each other.

Ephesians 2:22 And in Christ you, too, are being built together with the Jews into a place where God lives through the Spirit.

James 4:5 Do you think the Scripture means nothing that says, "The Spirit that God made to live in us wants us for himself alone?"

2 Corinthians 3:6 He made us able to be servants of a new agreement from himself to his people. This new agreement is not a written law, but it is of the Spirit. The written law brings death, but the Spirit gives life.

John 7:37-39 On the last and most important day of the feast Jesus stood up and said in a loud voice, "Let anyone who is thirsty come to me and drink. If anyone believes in me, rivers of living water will flow out from that person's heart, as the Scripture says." Jesus was talking about the Holy Spirit. The Spirit had not yet been given, because Jesus had not yet been raised to glory. But later, those who believed in Jesus would receive the Spirit.

Ephesians 5:18-20 Do not be drunk with wine, which will ruin you, but be filled with the Spirit. Speak to each other with psalms, hymns, and spiritual songs, singing and making music in your hearts to the Lord. Always give thanks to God the Father for everything, in the name of our Lord Jesus Christ.

Galatians 3:1-5 You people in Galatia were told very clearly about the death of Jesus Christ on the cross. But you were foolish; you let someone trick you. Tell me this one thing: How did you receive the Holy Spirit? Did you receive the Spirit by following the law? No, you received the Spirit because you heard the Good News and believed it. You began your life in Christ by the Spirit. Now are you trying to make it complete by your own power? That is foolish. Were all your experiences wasted? I hope not! Does God give you the Spirit and work miracles among you because you follow the law? No, he does these things because you heard the Good News and believed it.

God Uses Us To Spread His Knowledge:
Do Not Sell The Word Of God For Profit

2 Corinthians 2:14-17 But thanks be to God, who always leads us in victory through Christ. God uses us to spread his knowledge everywhere like a sweet-smelling perfume. Our offering to God is this: We are the sweet smell of Christ among those who are being saved and among those who are being lost. To those who are lost, we are the smell of death that brings death, but to those who are being saved, we are the smell of life that brings life. So who is able to do this work? We do not sell the word of God for a profit as many other people do. But in Christ we speak the truth before God, as messengers of God.

We Are Servants/Slaves Of Christ

1 Corinthians 4:1 People should think of us as servants of Christ, the ones God has trusted with his secrets.

2 Corinthians 4:5 We do not preach about ourselves, but we preach that Jesus Christ is Lord and that we are your servants for Jesus.

1 Corinthians 7:22-23 Those who were slaves when the Lord called them are free persons who belong to the Lord, In the same way, those who were free when they were called are now Christ's slaves. You all were bought at a great price, so do not become slaves of people.

Luke 17:7-10 "Suppose one of you has a servant who has been plowing the ground or caring for the sheep. When the servant comes in from working in the field, would you say, 'Come in and sit down to eat?' No, you would say to him, 'Prepare something for me to eat. Then get yourself ready and serve me. After I finish eating and drinking, you can eat.' The servant does not get any special thanks for doing what his master commanded. It is the same with you. When you have done everything you are told to do, you should say, 'We are unworthy servants; we have only done the work we should do.'"

2 Corinthians 3:6 He made us able to be servants of a new agreement from himself to his people. This new agreement is not written law, but it is the Spirit. The written law brings death, but the Spirit gives life.

Galatians 1:10 Do you think I am trying to make people accept me? No, God is the One I am trying to please. Am I trying to please people? If I still wanted to please people, I would not be a servant of Christ.

Ephesians 3:7 By God's special gift of grace given to me through his power, I became a servant to tell that Good News.

Ephesians 4:12 Christ gave those gifts to prepare God's holy people for the work of serving, to make the body of Christ stronger.

Colossians 3:24 Remember that you will receive your reward from the Lord, which he promised to his people. You are serving the Lord Christ.

1 Timothy 4:6-10 By telling these things to the brothers and sisters, you will be a good servant of Christ Jesus. You will be made strong by the words of the faith and the good teaching which you have been following. But do not follow foolish stories that disagree with God's truth, but train yourself to serve God. Training your body helps you in some ways, but serving God helps you in every way by bringing you blessings in this life and in the future life, too. What I say is true, and you should fully accept it. This is why we work and struggle: We hope in the living God who is the Savior of all people, especially of those who believe.

1 Peter 4:11 Anyone who speaks should speak words from God. Anyone who serves should serve with the strength God gives so that in everything God will be praised through Jesus Christ. Power and glory belong to him forever and ever. Amen.

1 Peter 2:16 Live as free people, but do not use your freedom as an excuse to do evil. Live as servants of God.

2 Peter 1:3 Jesus has the power of God, by which he has given us everything we need to live and to serve God. We have these things because we know him. Jesus called us by his glory and goodness.

Romans 6:19 I use this example because this is hard for you to understand. In the past you offered the parts of your body to be slaves to sin and evil; you lived only for evil. In the same way now you must give yourselves to be slaves of goodness. Then you will live only for God.

Romans 6:22 But now you are free from sin and have become slaves of God. This brings you a life that is only for God, and this gives you life forever.

Mark 10:43-45 "But it should not be that way among you. Whoever wants to become great among you must serve the rest of you like a servant. Whoever wants to become the first among you must serve all of you like a slave. In the same way, the Son of Man did not come to be served. He came to serve others and to give his life as a ransom for many people."

Mark 9:35 Jesus sat down and called the twelve apostles to him. He said, "Whoever wants to be the most important must be last of all and servant of all."

Luke 22:24-27 The apostles also began to argue about which one of them was the most important. But Jesus said to them, "The kings of the non-Jewish people rule over them, and those who have authority over others like to be called 'friends of the people.' But you must not be like that. Instead, the greatest among you should be like the youngest, and the leader should be like the servant.

Who is more important: the one sitting at the table or the one serving? You think the one at the table is more important, but I am like a servant among you."

2 Corinthians 6:6-7 We show we are servants of God by our pure lives, our understanding, patience, and kindness, by the Holy Spirit, by true love, by speaking the truth, and by God's power. We use our right living to defend ourselves against everything.

Philippians 2:7 But he gave up his place with God and made himself nothing.

> He was born to be a man
> and became like a servant.

Do Not Associate With Believers Who...

1 Corinthians 5:11-13 I am writing to tell you that you must not associate with those who call themselves believers in Christ but who sin sexually, or are greedy, or worship idols, or abuse others with words, or get drunk, or cheat people. Do not even eat with people like that.

It is not my business to judge those who are not part of the church. God will judge them. But you must judge the people who are part of the church. The Scripture says, "You must get rid of the evil person among you."

Christ Is The Rock/Stone

1 Corinthians 10:3-5 They all ate the same spiritual food, and all drank the same spiritual drink. They drank from that spiritual rock that followed them, and that rock was Christ. But God was not pleased with most of them, so they died in the desert.

Ephesians 2:20-22 You are like a building that was built on the foundation of the apostles and prophets. Christ Jesus himself is the most important stone in that building, and that whole building is joined together in Christ. He makes it grow and become a holy temple in the Lord. And in Christ you, too, are being built together with the Jews into a place where God lives through the Spirit.

1 Peter 2:4-8 Come to the Lord Jesus, the "stone" that lives. The people of the world did not want this stone, but he was the stone God chose, and he was precious. You also are like living stones, so let yourselves be used to build a spiritual temple—to be holy priests who offer spiritual sacrifices to God. He will accept those sacrifices through Jesus Christ. The Scripture says:

> "I will put a stone in the ground in Jerusalem.
> Everything will be built on this important and precious rock.
> Anyone who trusts in him
> will never be disappointed." (Isaiah 28:16)

This stone is worth much to you who believe. But to the people who do not believe,

> "the stone that the builders rejected
> has become the cornerstone." (Psalm 118:22)

Also, he is

> "a stone that causes people to stumble,
> a rock that makes them fall." (Isaiah 8:14)

They stumble because they do not obey what God says, which is what God planned to happen to them.

Matthew 16:18 "So I tell you, you are Peter. On this rock I will build my church, and the power of death will not be able to defeat it."

Romans 9:31-33 The people of Israel tried to follow a law to make themselves right with God. But they did not succeed, because they tried to make themselves right by the things they did instead of trusting in God to make them right. They stumbled over the stone that causes people to stumble. As it is written in the Scripture:

> "I will put in Jerusalem a stone that causes people
> to stumble,
> a rock that makes them fall.
> Anyone who trusts in him will never be
> disappointed." (Isaiah 8:14; 28:16)

Give Thanks To God In The Name Of Our Lord Jesus: If You Do Anything, Do It For The Glory Of God: If You Ask For Anything, Ask For It In Jesus' Name

1 Peter 4:11 Anyone who speaks should speak words from God. Anyone who serves should serve with the strength God gives so that in everything God will be praised through Jesus Christ. Power and glory belong to him forever and ever. Amen.

John 14:11-14 "Believe me when I say that I am in the Father and the Father is in me. Or believe because of the miracles I have done. I tell you the truth, whoever believes in me will do the same things that I do. Those who believe will do even greater things than these, because I am going to the Father. And if you ask for anything in my name, I will do it for you so that the Father's glory will be shown through the Son. If you ask me for anything in my name, I will do it."

1 Corinthians 10:31-33 The answer is, if you eat or drink, or if you do anything, do it all for the glory of God. Never do anything that might hurt others—Jews, Greeks, or God's church—just as I, also, try to please everybody in every way. I am not trying to do what is good for me but what is good for most people so they can be saved.

Ephesians 5:19-20 Speak to each other with psalms, hymns, and spiritual songs, singing and making music in your hearts to the Lord. Always give thanks to God the Father for everything, in the name of our Lord Jesus Christ.

Colossians 3:17 Everything you do or say should be done to obey Jesus your Lord. And in all you do, give thanks to God the Father through Jesus.

John 16:26 "In that day you will ask the Father for things in my name. I mean, I will not need to ask the Father for you."

When You Suffer For Christ, You Are Strong

2 Corinthians 12:9-10 But he said to me, "My grace is enough for you. When you are weak, my power is made perfect in you." So I am very happy to brag about my weaknesses. Then Christ's power can live in me. For this reason I am happy when I have weaknesses, insults, hard times, sufferings, and all kings of troubles for Christ. Because when I am weak, then I am truly strong.

1 Peter 2:20-25 If you are beaten for doing wrong, there is no reason to praise you for being patient in your punishment. But if you suffer for doing good, and you are patient, then God is pleased. This is what you were called to do, because Christ suffered for you and gave you an example to follow. So you should do as he did.

> "He had never sinned,
> and he had never lied." (Isaiah 53:9)

People insulted Christ, but he did not insult them in return. Christ suffered, but he did not threaten. He let God, the One who judges rightly, take care of him. Christ carried our sins in his body on the cross so we would stop living for sin and start living for what is right. And you are healed because of his wounds. You were like sheep that wandered away, but now you have come back to the Shepherd and Protector of your souls.

1 Peter 4:1-2 Since Christ suffered while he was in his body, strengthen yourselves with the same way of thinking Christ had. The person who has suffered in the body is finished with sin. Strengthen yourselves so that you will live here on earth doing what God wants, not the evil things people want.

1 Peter 4:12-19 My friends, do not be surprised at the terrible trouble which now comes to test you. Do not think that something strange is happening to you. But be happy that you are sharing in Christ's sufferings so that you will be happy and full of joy when Christ comes again in glory. When people insult you because you follow Christ, you are blessed, because the glorious Spirit, the Spirit of God, is with you. Do not suffer for murder, theft, or any other crime, nor because you trouble other people. But if you suffer because you are a Christian, do not be ashamed. Praise God because you wear that name. It is time for judgment to begin with God's family. And if that judging begins with us, what will happen to those people who do not obey the Good News of God?

"If it is very hard for a good person to be saved,

the wicked person and the sinner will surely be lost!"

So those who suffer as God wants should trust their souls to the faithful Creator as they continue to do what is right.

Love

1 Corinthians 13:4-13 Love is patient and kind. Love is not jealous, it does not brag, and it is not proud, Love is not rude, is not selfish, and does not get upset with others. Love does not count up wrongs that have been done. Love is not happy with evil but is happy with the truth. Love patiently accepts all things. It always trusts, always hopes, and always remains strong.

Love never ends. There are gifts of prophecy, but they will be ended. There are gifts of speaking in different languages, but those gifts will stop. There is the gift of knowledge, but it will come to an end. The reason is that our knowledge and our ability to prophesy are not perfect. But when perfection comes, the things that are not perfect will end. When I was a child, I talked like a child, I thought like a child, I reasoned like a child. When I became a man, I stopped those childish ways. It is the same with us. Now we see a dim reflection, as if we were looking into a mirror, but then we shall see clearly. Now I know only a part, but then I will know fully, as God has known me. So these three things continue forever: faith, hope, and love. And the greatest of these is love.

Tongues

1 Corinthians 14:1-28 You should seek after love, and you should truly want to have the spiritual gifts, especially the gift of prophecy. I will explain why. Those who have the gift of speaking in different languages are not speaking to people; they are speaking to God. No one understands them; they are speaking secret things through the Spirit. But those who prophesy are speaking to people to give them strength, encouragement, and comfort. The ones who speak in different languages are helping only themselves, but those who prophesy are helping the whole church. I wish all of you had the gift of speaking in different kinds of languages, but more, I wish you would prophesy. Those who prophesy are greater than those who can only speak in different languages—unless someone is there who can explain what is said so that the whole church can be helped.

Brothers and sisters, will it help you if I come to you speaking in different languages? No! It will help you only if I bring you a new truth or some new knowledge, or prophecy, or teaching. It is the same as with lifeless things that make sounds—like a flute or a harp. If they do not make clear musical notes, you will not know what is being played. And in a war, if the trumpet does not give a clear sound, who will prepare for battle? It is the same with you. Unless you speak clearly with your tongue, no one can understand what you are saying. You will be talking into the air! It may be true that there are all kinds of sounds in the world, and none is without meaning. But unless I understand the meaning of what someone says to me, I will be a foreigner to him, and he will be a foreigner to me. It is the same with you. Since you want spiritual gifts very much, seek most of all to have the gifts that help the church grow stronger.

The one who has the gift of speaking in a different language should pray for the gift to interpret what is spoken. If I pray in a different language, my spirit is praying, but my mind does nothing. So what should I do? I will pray with my spirit, but I will also pray with my mind. I will sing with my spirit, but will also sing with my mind. If you praise God with your spirit, those persons there without understanding cannot say amen to your prayer of thanks, because they do not know what you are saying. You may be thanking God in a good way, but the other person is not helped.

I thank God that I speak in different kings of languages more than all of you. But in the church meetings I would rather speak five words I understand in order to teach others than thousands of words in a different language.

Brothers and sisters, do not think like children. In evil things be like babies, but in your thinking you should be like adults. It is written in the Scriptures:

"With people who use strange words and foreign languages
I will speak to these people.
But even then they will not listen to me," (Isaiah 28:11-12)
Says the Lord.

So the gift of speaking in different kinds of languages is a proof for those who do not believe, not for those who do believe. And prophecy is for people who believe, not for those who do not believe. Suppose the whole church meets together and everyone speaks in different languages. If some people come in who do not understand or do not believe, they will say you are crazy. But suppose everyone is prophesying and some people come in who do not believe or do not understand. If everyone is prophesying, their sin will be shown to them, and they will be judged by all that they hear. The secret things in their hearts will be made known. So they will bow down and worship God saying, "Truly, God is with you."

So, brothers and sisters, what should you do? When you meet together, one person has a song, and another has a teaching. Another has a new truth from God. Another speaks in a different language, and another person interprets that language. The purpose of all these things should be to help the church grow strong. When you meet together, if anyone speaks in a different language, it should be only two, or not more than three, who speak. They should speak one after the other, and someone else should interpret. But if there is no interpreter, then those who speak in a different language should be quiet in the church meeting. They should speak only to themselves and to God.

1 Corinthians 14:33 God is not a God of Confusion but a God of peace.

1 Corinthians 14:39-40 So my brothers and sisters, you should truly want to prophesy. But do not stop people from using the gift of speaking in different kinds of languages. But let everything be done in a right and orderly way.

1 Corinthians 12:30 Not all have gifts of healing. Not all speak in different languages. Not all interpret those languages.

Women In Church Meetings

1 Corinthians 14:33-35 God is not a God of confusion but a God of peace.

As is true in all the churches of God's people, women should keep quiet in the church meetings. They are not allowed to speak, but they must yield to this rule as the law says. If they want to learn something, they should ask their own husbands at home. It is shameful for a woman to speak in the church meeting.

1 Timothy 2:11-15 Let a woman learn by listening quietly and being ready to cooperate in everything. But I do not allow a woman to teach or to have authority over a man, but to listen quietly, because Adam was formed first and then Eve. And Adam was not tricked, but the woman was tricked and became a sinner. But she will be saved through having children if they continue in faith, love, and holiness, with self-control

Physical Bodies First, Then The Spiritual

1 Corinthians 15:44-58 The body that is "planted" is a physical body. When it is raised, it is a spiritual body.

There is a physical body, and there is also a spiritual body. It is written in the Scriptures: "The first man, Adam, became a living person." But the last Adam became a spirit that gives life. The spiritual did not come first, but the physical and then the spiritual. The first man came from the dust of the earth. The second man came from heaven. People who belong to the earth are like the first man of earth. But those people who belong to heaven are like the man of heaven. Just as we were made like the man of earth, so we will also be made like the man of heaven.

I tell you this, brothers and sisters: Flesh and blood cannot have a part in the kingdom of God. Something that will ruin cannot have a part in something that never ruins. But look! I tell you this secret: We will not all sleep in death, but we will all be changed. It will take only a second—as quickly as an eye blinks—when the last trumpet sounds. The trumpet will sound, and those who have died will be raised to live forever, and we will all be changed. This body that can be destroyed must clothe itself with something that can never be destroyed. And this body that dies must clothe itself with something that can never die. So this body that can be destroyed will clothe itself with that which can never be destroyed, and this body that dies will clothe itself with that which can never die. When this happens, this Scripture will be made true:

> "Death is destroyed forever in victory." (Isaiah 25:8)
> "Death, where is your victory?
> Death, where is your pain?" (Hosea 13:14)

Death's power to hurt is sin, and the power of sin is the law. But we thank God! He gives us the victory through our Lord Jesus Christ.

So my dear brothers and sisters, stand strong. Do not let anything change you. Always give yourselves fully to the work of the Lord, because you know that your work in the Lord is never wasted.

Death's Power To Hurt Is Sin And The
Power Of Sin Is The Law

1 Corinthians 15:56-57 Death's power to hurt is sin, and the power of sin is the law. But we thank God! He gives us the victory through our Lord Jesus Christ.

Galatians 2:17-21 We Jews came to Christ, trying to be made right with God, and it became clear that we are sinners, too. Does this mean that Christ encourages sin? No! But I would really be wrong to begin teaching again those things that I gave up. It was the law that put me to death, and I died to the law so that I can now live for God. I was put to death on the cross with Christ, and I do not live anymore—it is Christ who lives in me. I still live in my body, but I live by faith in the Son of God who loved me and gave himself to save me. By saying these things I am not going against God's grace. Just the opposite, if the law could make us right with God, then Christ's death would be useless.

Jesus Christ Will Judge Us By How We Used
Our Body (Tent) Here On Earth

2 Corinthians 5:1-10 We know that our body—the tent we live in here on earth—will be destroyed. But when that happens, God will have a house for us. It will not be a house made my human hands; instead, it will be a home in heaven that will last forever. But now we groan in this tent. We want God to give us our heavenly home, because it will clothe us so we will not be naked. While we live in this body, we have burdens, and we groan. We do not want to be naked, but we want to be clothed with our heavenly home. Then this body that dies will be fully covered with life. This is what God made us for, and he has given us the Spirit to be a guarantee for this new life.

So we always have courage. We know that while we live in this body, we are away from the Lord. We live by what we believe, not by what we can see. So I say that we have courage. We really want to be away from this body and be at home with the Lord. Our only goal is to please God whether we live here or there, because we must all stand before Christ to be judged. Each of us will receive what we should get—good or bad—for the things we did in the earthy body.

Matthew 25:14-30 "The kingdom of heaven is like a man who was going to another place for a visit. Before he left, he called for his servants and told them to take care of his things while he was gone. He gave one servant five bags of gold, another servant two bags of gold, and a third servant one bag of gold, to each one as much as he could handle. Then he left. The servant who got five bags went quickly to invest the money and earned five more bags. In the same way, the servant who had two bags invested them and earned two more. The servant who got one bag went out and dug a hole in the ground and hid the master's money.

"After a long time the master came home and asked the servants what they did with his money. The servant who was given five bags of gold brought five more bags to the master and said, 'Master, you trusted me to care for five bags of gold, so I used your five bags to earn five more.' The master answered, 'You did well. You are a good and loyal servant. Because you were loyal with small things, I will let you care for much greater things. Come and share my joy with me.'

"Then the servant who had been given two bags of gold came to the master and said, 'Master, you gave me two bags of gold to care for, so I used your two bags to earn two more.' The master answered, 'You did well. You are a good and loyal servant. Because you were loyal with small things, I will let you care for much greater things. Come and share my joy with me.'

"Then the servant who had been given one bag of gold came to the master and said, 'Master, I knew that you were a hard man. You harvest things you did not plant. You gather crops where you did not sow any seed. So I was afraid and went and hid your money in the ground. Here is your bag of gold.' The master answered, 'You are a wicked and lazy servant! You say you knew that I harvest things I did not plant and that I gather crops where I did not sow any seed. So you should have put my gold in the bank. Then, when I came home, I would have received my gold back with interest.'

"So the master told his other servants, 'Take the bag of gold from that servant and give it to the servant who has ten bags of gold. Those who have much will get more, and they will have much more than they need. But those who do not have much will have everything taken away from them.' Then the master said, 'Throw that useless servant outside, into the darkness where people will cry and grind their teeth with pain.'"

Luke 19:11-27 Same as above with variations. (A coin is used instead of gold)

This is a story about three servants and how each was judged by how they used God's wealth, bag(s) of gold. God expects us to use His wealth. Some of the wealth he gives us is Salvation; The Word; Time; Prayer; etc. The Lord will ask for an accounting. How we use the wealth of God is how we will be judged. Matthew 25:35-36 "'I was hungry, and you gave me food. I was thirsty, and you gave me something to drink. I was alone and away from home, and you invited me into your house. I was without clothes, and you gave me something to wear. I was sick, and you cared for me. I was in prison, and you visited me.'"

Hebrews 4:13 Nothing in all the world can be hidden from God. Everything is clear and lies open before him, and to him we must explain the way we have lived.

Elders And Deacons

1 Timothy 3:1-16 What I say is true: Anyone wanting to become an elder desires a good work. An elder must not give people a reason to criticize him, and he must have only one wife....

In the same way, deacons must be respected by others, not saying things they do not mean....

Christians Should Not Be Like This:
The Spirit Produces The Fruit Of ...

2 Corinthians 12:20-21 I am afraid that when I come, you will not be what I want you to be, and I will not be what you want me to be. I am afraid that among you there may be arguing, jealousy, anger, selfish fighting, evil talk, gossip, pride, and confusion. I am afraid that when I come to you again, my God will make me ashamed before you. I may be saddened by many of those who have sinned because they have not changed their hearts or turned from their sexual sins and the shameful things they have done.

Galatians 5:19-26 The wrong things the sinful self does are clear: being sexually unfaithful, not being pure, taking part in sexual sins, worshiping gods, doing witchcraft, hating, making trouble, being jealous, being angry, being selfish, making people angry with each other, causing division among people, feeling envy, being drunk, having wild and wasteful parties, and doing other things like these. I warn you now as I warned you before: Those who do these things will not inherit God's kingdom. But the Spirit produces the fruit of love, joy, peace, patience, kindness, goodness, faithfulness, gentleness, self-control. There is no law that says these things are wrong. Those who belong to Christ Jesus have crucified their own sinful selves. They have given up their old selfish feelings and the evil things they wanted to do. We get our new life from the Spirit, so we should follow the Spirit. We must not be proud or make trouble with each other or be jealous of each other.

1 Peter 5:5-6 In the same way, younger people should be willing to be under older people. And all of you should be very humble with each other.

> "God is against the proud,
> but he gives grace to the humble." (Proverbs 3:34)

Be humble under God's powerful hand so he will lift you up when the right time comes. Give all your worries to him, because he cares about you.

Matthew 12:33-37 "If you want good fruit, you must make the tree good. If your tree is not good, it will have bad fruit. A tree is known by the kind of fruit it produces. You snakes! You are evil people, so how can you say anything good? The mouth speaks the things that are in the heart. Good people have good things in their hearts, and so they say good things. But evil people have evil in their hearts, so they say evil things. And I tell you that on the Judgment Day people will be responsible for every careless thing they have said. The words you have said will be used to judge you. Some of your words will prove you right, but some of your words will prove you guilty."

Don't Think Jesus Came To Bring Peace To Earth, But A Sword

Matthew 10:34-40 "Don't think that I came to bring peace to the earth. I did not come to bring peace, but a sword. I have come so that

> 'a son will be against his father,
> a daughter will be against her mother,
> a daughter-in-law will be against her mother-in-law.
> A person's enemies will be members of his own family.' (Micah 7:6)

"Those who love their father or mother more than they love me are not worthy to be my followers. Those who love their son or daughter more than they love me are not worthy to be my followers. Whoever is not willing to carry the cross and follow me is not worthy of me. Those who try to hold on to their lives will give up true life. Those who give up their lives for me will hold on to true life. Whoever accepts you also accepts me, and whoever accepts me also accepts the One who sent me.

Hebrews 4:12-13 God's word is alive and working and is sharper than a double-edged sword. It cuts all the way into us, where the soul and the spirit are joined, to the center of our joints and bones. And it judges the thoughts and feelings in our hearts. Nothing in all the world can be hidden from God. Everything is clear and lies open before him, and to him we must explain the way we have lived.

Ephesians 6:17 Accept God's salvation as your helmet, and take the sword of the spirit, which is the word of God.

2 Timothy 3:16-17 All Scripture is given by God and is useful for teaching, for showing people what is wrong in their lives, for correcting faults, and for teaching how to live right. Using the Scriptures, the person who serves God will be capable, having all that is needed to do every good work.

Luke 12:49-53 "I came to set fire to the world, and I wish it were already burning! I have a baptism to suffer through, and I feel very troubled until it is over. Do you think I came to give peace to the earth? No, I tell you, I came to divide it. From now on, a family with five people will be divided, three against two, and two against three. They will be divided: father against son and son against father, mother against daughter and daughter against mother, mother-in-law against daughter-in-law and daughter-in-law against mother-in-law."

Today, God Speaks Through Jesus

Hebrews 1:1-4 In the past God spoke to our ancestors through the prophets many times and in many different ways. But now in these last days God has spoken to us through his Son. God has chosen his Son to own all things, and through him he made the world. The Son reflects the glory of God and shows exactly what God is like. He holds everything together with his powerful word. When the Son made people clean from their sins, he sat down at the right side of God, the Great One in heaven. The Son became much greater than the angels, and God gave him a name that is much greater than theirs.

God's Word Is Sharper Than A Double-Edged Sword

Hebrews 4:12-13 God's word is alive and working and is sharper than a double-edged sword. It cuts all the way into us, where the soul and the spirit are joined, to the center of our joints and bones. And it judges the thoughts and feelings in our hearts. Nothing in all the world can be hidden from God. Everything is clear and lies open before him, and to him we must explain the way we have lived.

Ephesians 6:17 Accept God's salvation as your helmet, and take the sword of the Spirit, which is the word of God.

2 Timothy 3:16-17 All Scripture is given by God and is useful for teaching, for showing people what is wrong in their lives, for correcting faults, and for teaching how to live right. Using the Scriptures, the person who serves God will be capable, having all that is needed to do every good work.

Matthew 10:34-40 "Don't think that I came to bring peace to the earth. I did not come to bring peace, but a sword. I have come so that

> 'a son will be against his father,
> a daughter will be against her mother,
> a daughter-in-law will be against her mother-in-law.
> A person's enemies will be members of his own family.' (Micah 7:6)

"Those who love their father or mother more than they love me are not worthy to be my followers. Those who love their son or daughter more than they love me are not worthy to be my followers. Whoever is not willing to carry the cross and follow me is not worthy of me. Those who try to hold on to their lives will give up true life. Those who give up their lives for me will hold on to true life. Whoever accepts you also accepts me, and whoever accepts me also accepts the One who sent me.

Why Don't We Always Get What We Ask God For?

James 4:1-10 Do you know where your fights and arguments come from? They come from the selfish desires that war within you. You want things, but you do not have them. So you are ready to kill and are jealous of other people, but you still cannot get what you want. So you argue and fight. You do not get what you want, because you do not ask God. Or when you ask, you do not receive because the reason you ask is wrong. You want things so you can use them for your own pleasures.

So, you are not loyal to God! You should know that loving the world is the same as hating God. Anyone who wants to be a friend of the world becomes God's enemy. Do you think the Scripture means nothing that says, "The Spirit that God made to live in us wants us for himself alone?" But God gives us even more grace, as the Scripture says,

> "God is against the proud,
> but he gives grace to the humble." (Proverbs 3:34)

So give yourselves completely to God. Stand against the devil, and the devil will run from you. Come near to God, and God will come near to you. You sinners, clean sin out of your lives. You who are trying to follow God and the world at the same time, make your thinking pure. Be sad, cry, and weep! Change your laughter into crying and your joy into sadness. Don't be too proud in the Lord's presence, and he will make you great.

1 John 5:14-15 And this is the boldness we have in God's presence: that if we ask God for anything that agrees with what he wants, he hears us. If we know he hears us every time we ask him, we know we have what we ask from him.

1 John 3:22-24 And God gives us what we ask for because we obey God's commands and do what pleases him. This is what God commands: that we believe in his Son, Jesus Christ, and that we love each other, just as he commanded. The people who obey God's commands live in God, and God lives in them. We know that God lives in us because of the Spirit God gave us.

Luke 18:6-8 The Lord said, "Listen to what the unfair judge said. God will always give what is right to his people who cry to him night and day, and he will not be slow to answer them. I tell you, God will help his people quickly. But when the Son of Man comes again, will he find those on earth who believe in him?"

John 14:13-14 "And if you ask for anything in my name, I will do it for you so that the Father's glory will be shown through the Son. If you ask me for anything in my name, I will do it."

John 15:7-8 "If you remain in me and follow my teachings, you can ask anything you want, and it will be given to you. You should produce much fruit and show that you are my followers, which brings glory to my Father."

Matthew 21:21-22 Jesus answered, "I tell you the truth, if you have faith and do not doubt, you will be able to do what I did to this tree and even more. You will be able to say to this mountain, 'Go, fall into the sea.' And if you have faith, it will happen. If you believe, you will get anything you ask for in prayer."

James 1:6-8 But when you ask God, you must believe and not doubt. Anyone who doubts is like a wave in the sea, blown up and down by the wind. Such doubters are thinking two different things at the same time, and they cannot decide about anything they do. They should not think they will receive anything from the Lord.

James 1:2-3 My brothers and sisters, when you have many kinds of troubles, you should be full of joy, because you know that these troubles test your faith, and this will give you patience.

1 Peter 1:5-9 God's power protects you through your faith until salvation is shown to you at the end of time. This makes you very happy, even though now for a short time different kinds of troubles may make you sad. These troubles come to prove that your faith is pure. This purity of faith is worth more than gold, which can be proved to be pure by fire but will ruin. But the purity of your faith will bring you praise and glory and honor when Jesus Christ is shown to you. You have not seen Christ, but still you love him. You cannot see him now, but you believe in him. So you are filled with a joy that cannot be explained, a joy full of glory. And you are receiving the goal of your faith—the salvation of your souls.

Mark 11:22-26 Jesus answered, "Have faith in God. I tell you the truth, you can say to this mountain, 'Go, fall into the sea.' And if you have no doubts in your mind and believe that what you say will happen, God will do it for you. So I tell you to believe that you have received the things you ask for in prayer, and God will give them to you. When you are praying, if you are angry with someone, forgive him so that your Father in heaven will also forgive your sins."

Rich People

James 5:1-6 You rich people, listen! Cry and be very sad because of the troubles that are coming to you. Your riches have rotted, and your clothes have been eaten by moths. Your gold and silver have rusted, and that rust will be a proof that you were wrong. It will eat your bodies like fire. You saved your treasure for the last days. The pay you did not give the workers who mowed your fields cries out against you, and the cries of the workers have been heard by the Lord All Powerful. Your life on earth was full of rich living and pleasing yourselves with everything you wanted. You made yourselves fat, like an animal ready to be killed. You have judged guilty and then murdered innocent people, who were not against you.

Matthew 19:21-26 Jesus answered, "If you want to be perfect, then go and sell your possessions and give the money to the poor. If you do this, you will have treasure in heaven. Then come and follow me."

But when the young man heard this, he left sorrowfully, because he was rich.

Then Jesus said to his followers, "I tell you the truth, it will be hard for a rich person to enter the kingdom of heaven. Yes, I tell you that it is easier for a camel to go through the eye of a needle than for a rich person to enter the kingdom of God."

When Jesus' followers heard this, they were very surprised and asked, "Then who can be saved?"

Jesus looked at them and said, "This is something people cannot do, but God can do all things."

Luke 6:24-26 "But how terrible it will be for you who are rich,

> because you have had your easy life.
> How terrible it will be for you who are full now,
> because you will be hungry.
> How terrible it will be for you who are laughing now,
> because you will be sad and cry.

"How terrible when everyone says only good things about you, because their ancestors said the same things about the false prophets."

James 2:5-7 Listen, my dear brothers and sister! God chose the poor in the world to be rich with faith and to receive the kingdom God promised to those who love him. But you show no respect to the poor. The rich are always trying to control your lives. They are the ones who take you to court. And they are the ones who speak against Jesus, who owns you.

I Timothy 6:6-10 Serving God does make us very rich, if we are satisfied with what we have. We brought nothing into the world, so we can take nothing out. But, if we have food and clothes, we will be satisfied with that. Those who want to become rich bring temptation to themselves and are caught in a trap. They want many foolish and harmful things that ruin and destroy people. The love of money causes all kinds of evil. Some people have left the faith, because they wanted to get more money, but they have caused themselves much sorrow.

No Fear

1 John 4:17-18 This is how love is made perfect in us: that we can be without fear on the day God judges us, because in this world we are like him. Where God's love is, there is no fear, because God's perfect love drives out fear. It is punishment that makes a person fear, so love is not made perfect in the person who fears.

1 John 3:19-21 This is the way we know that we belong to the way of truth. When our hearts make us feel guilty, we can still have peace before God. God is greater than our hearts, and he knows everything. My dear friends, if our hearts do not make us feel guilty, we can come without fear into God's presence.

Hebrews 2:14-15 Since these children are people with physical bodies, Jesus himself became like them. He did this so that, by dying, he could destroy the one who has the power of death—the devil—and free those who were like slaves all their lives because of their fear of death.

2 Timothy 1:7 God did not give us a spirit that makes us afraid but a spirit of power and love and self-control.

Hebrews 13:6 So we can be sure when we say,

> "I will not be afraid, because the Lord is my helper.
> People can't do anything to me." (Psalm 118:6)

Romans 8:15 The Spirit we received does not make us slaves again to fear; it makes us children of God. With that Spirit we cry out, "Father."

Freedom Through Christ

1 Peter 2:16-17 Live as free people, but do not use your freedom as an excuse to do evil. Live as servants of God. Show respect for all people: Love the brothers and sisters of God's family, respect God, honor the king.

2 Corinthians 3:17 The Lord is the Spirit, and where the Sprit of the Lord is, there is freedom.

Galatians 5:1 We have freedom now, because Christ made us free. So stand strong. Do not change and go back into the slavery of the law.

Hebrews 2:14-15 Since these children are people with physical bodies, Jesus himself became like them. He did this so that, by dying, he could destroy the one who has the power of death—the devil—and free those who were like slaves all their lives because of their fear of death.

Romans 8:2 Through Christ Jesus the law of the Spirit that brings life made me free from the law that brings sin and death.

Hebrews 9:15 For this reason Christ brings a new agreement from God to his people. Those who are called by God can now receive the blessings he has promised, blessings that will last forever. They can have those things because Christ died so that the people who lived under the first agreement could be set free from sin.

1 Corinthians 8:9 But be careful that your freedom does not cause those who are weak in faith to fall into sin.

Galatians 5:13 My brothers and sisters, God called you to be free, but do not use your freedom as an excuse to do what pleases your sinful self. Serve each other with love.

You Are A Slave To Anything That Controls You

2 Peter 2:19 They promise them freedom, but they themselves are not free. They are slaves of things that will be destroyed. For people are slaves of anything that controls them.

False Teachers

2 Peter 2:1-3 There used to be false prophets among God's people, just as you will have some false teachers in your group. They will secretly teach things that are wrong—teachings that will cause people to be lost. They will even refuse to accept the Master, Jesus, who bought their freedom. So they will bring quick ruin on themselves. Many will follow their evil ways and say evil things about the way of truth. Those false teachers only want your money, so they will use you by telling you lies. Their judgment spoken against them long ago is still coming, and their ruin is certain.

2 Peter 2:9-22 So the Lord knows how to save those who serve him when troubles come. **He will hold evil people and punish them, while waiting for the Judgment Day.** That punishment is especially for those who live by doing the evil things their sinful selves want and who hate authority.

These false teachers are bold and do anything they want. They are not afraid to speak against the angels. But even the angels, who are much stronger and more powerful than false teachers, do not accuse them with insults before the Lord. But these people speak against things they do not understand. They are like animals that act without thinking, animals born to be caught and killed. And, like animals, these false teachers will be destroyed. They have caused many people to suffer, so they themselves will suffer. That is their pay for what they have done. They take pleasure in openly doing evil, so they are like dirty spots and stains among you. They delight in trickery while eating meals with you. Every time they look at a woman they want her, and their desire for sin is never satisfied. They lead weak people into the trap of sin, and they have taught their hearts to be greedy. God will punish them! These false teachers left the right road and lost their way, following the way Balaam went. Balaam was the son of Beor, who loved being paid for doing wrong. But a donkey, which cannot talk, told Balaam he was sinning. It spoke with a man's voice and stopped the prophet's crazy thinking.

Those false teachers are like springs without water and clouds blown by a storm. A place in the blackest darkness has been kept for them. They brag with words that mean nothing. By their evil desires they lead people into the trap of sin—people who are just beginning to escape from others who live in error. They promise them freedom, but they themselves are not free. They are slaves of things that will be destroyed. For people are slaves of anything that controls them. They were made free from the evil in the world by knowing our Lord and Savior Jesus Christ. But if they return to evil things and those things control them, then it is worse for them than it was before. Yes, it would be better for them to have never known the right way than to know it and to turn away from the holy teaching that was given to them. What they did is like this true saying: "A dog goes back to what it has thrown up," and, "After a pig is washed, it goes back and rolls in the mud."

2 John 7-11 Many false teachers are in the world now who do not confess that Jesus Christ came to earth as a human. Anyone who does not confess this is a false teacher and an enemy of Christ. Be careful yourselves that you do not lose everything you have worked for, but that you receive your full reward.

Anyone who goes beyond Christ's teaching and does not continue to follow only his teaching does not have God. But whoever continues to follow the teaching of Christ has both the Father and the Son. If someone comes to you and does not bring this teaching, do not welcome or accept that person into your house. If you welcome such a person, you share in the evil work.

If We Say We Have Not Sinned, We Make God A Liar: Sin Comes From The Ways Of The World, Not The Father

1 John 1:10 If we say we have not sinned, we make God a liar, and we do not accept God's teaching.

1 John 2:16-17 These are the ways of the world: wanting to please our sinful selves, wanting the sinful things we see, and being too proud of what we have. None of these come from the Father, but all of them come from the world. The world and everything that people want in it are passing away, but the person who does what God wants lives forever.

Love Comes From God

1 John 4:7-21 Dear friends, we should love each other, because love comes from God. Everyone who loves has become God's child and knows God. Whoever does not love does not know God, because God is love. This is how God showed his love to us: He sent his one and only son into the world so that we could have life through him. This is what real love is: It is not our love for God; it is God's love for us in sending his Son to be the way to take away our sins.

Dear friends, if God loved us that much we also should love each other. No one has ever seen God, but if we love each other, God lives in us, and his love is made perfect in us.

We know that we live in God and he lives in us, because he gave us his Spirit. We have seen and can testify that the Father sent his Son to be the Savior of the world. Whoever confesses that Jesus is the Son of God has God living inside, and that person lives in God. And so we know the love that God has for us, and we trust that love.

God is love. Those who live in love live in God, and God lives in them. This is how love is made perfect in us: that we can be without fear on the day God judges us. Because in this world we are like him. Where God's love is, there is no fear, because God's perfect love drives out fear. It is punishment that makes a person fear, so love is not made perfect in the person who fears.

We love because God first loved us. If people say, "I love God," but hate their brothers or sisters, they are liars. Those who do not love their brothers and sisters, whom they have seen, cannot love God, whom they have never seen. And God gave us this command: Those who love God must also love their brothers and sisters.

Don't Call People On Earth Father

Matthew 23:8-12 "But you must not be called 'Teacher,' because you have only one Teacher, and you are all brothers and sisters together. And don't call any person on earth 'Father,' because you have one Father, who is in heaven. And you should not be called 'Master,' because you have only one Master, the Christ. Whoever is your servant is the greatest among you. Whoever makes himself great will be made humble. Whoever makes himself humble will be made great."

Grace

Romans 5:15-21 But God's free gift is not like Adam's sin. Many people died because of the sin of that one man. But the grace from God was much greater; many people received God's gift of life by the grace of the one man, Jesus Christ. After Adam sinned once, he was judged guilty. But the gift of God is different. God's free gift came after many sins, and it makes people right with God. One man sinned, and so death ruled all people because of that one man. But now those people who accept God's full grace and the great gift of being made right with him will surely have true life and rule through the one man, Jesus Christ.

So as one sin of Adam brought the punishment of death to all people, one good act that Christ did makes all people right with God. And that brings true life for all. One man disobeyed God, and many became sinners. In the same way, one man obeyed God, and many will be made right. The law came to make sin worse. But when sin grew worse, God's grace increased. Sin once used death to rule us, but God gave people more of his grace so that grace could rule by making people right with him. And this brings life forever through Jesus our Lord.

Romans 5:1-2 Since we have been made right with God by our faith, we have peace with God. This happened through our Lord Jesus Christ, who has brought us into that blessing of God's grace that we now enjoy. And we are happy because of the hope we have of sharing God's glory.

Romans 11:5-6 It is the same now. There are a few people that God has chosen by his grace. And if he chose them by grace, it is not for the things they have done. If they could be made God's people by what they did, God's gift of grace would not really be a gift.

Romans 12:6 We all have different gifts, each of which came because of the grace God gave us. The person who has the gift of prophecy should use that gift in agreement with the faith.

Ephesians 2:8-10 I mean that you have been saved by grace through believing. You did not save yourselves; it was a gift from God. It was not the result of your own efforts, so you cannot brag about it. God has made us what we are. In Christ Jesus, God made us to do good works, which God planned in advance for us to live our lives doing.

Ephesians 3:7 By God's special gift of grace given to me through his power, I became a servant to tell that Good News.

Acts 15:11 "But we believe that we and they too will be saved by the grace of the Lord Jesus."

James 4:5-6 Do you think the Scripture means nothing that says, "The Spirit that God made to live in us wants us for himself alone?" But God gives us even more grace, as the Scripture says,

> "God is against the proud,
> but he gives grace to the humble." (Proverbs 3:34)

John 1:14-18 The Word became a human and lived among us. We saw his glory—the glory that belongs to the only Son of the Father—and he was full of grace and truth. John tells the truth about him and cries out, saying, "This is the One I told you about: 'The One who comes after me is greater than I am, because he was living before me.'"
Because he was full of grace and truth, from him we all received one gift after another. The law was given through Moses, but grace and truth came through Jesus Christ. No one has ever seen God. But God the only Son is very close to the Father, and he has shown us what God is like.

2 Corinthians 6:1-2 We are workers together with God, so we beg you: Do not let the grace that you received from God be for nothing, God says,

> "At the right time I heard your prayers.
> On the day of salvation I helped you." (Isaiah 49:8)

I tell you that the "right time" is now, and the "day of salvation" is now.

1 Corinthians 15:9-10 All the other apostles are greater than I am. I am not even good enough to be called an apostle, because I persecuted the church of God. But God's grace has made me what I am, and his grace to me was not wasted. I worked harder than all the other apostles. (But it was not I really; it was God's grace that was with me.)

Acts 20:24 I don't care about my own life. The most important thing is that I complete my mission, the work that the Lord Jesus gave me—to tell people the Good News about God's grace.

Hebrews 2:9 But we see Jesus, who for a short time was made lower than the angels. And now he is wearing a crown of glory and honor because he suffered and died. And by God's grace, he died for everyone.

Hebrews 4:14-16 Since we have a great high priest, Jesus the Son of God, who has gone into heaven, let us hold on to the faith we have. For our high priest is able to understand our weaknesses. When he lived on earth, he was tempted in every way that we are, but he did not sin. Let us, then, feel very sure that we can come before God's throne where there is grace. There we can receive mercy and grace to help us when we need it.

Romans 6:14 Sin will not be your master, because you are not under law but under God's grace.

Galatians 5:4 If you try to be made right with God through the law, your life with Christ is over—you have left God's grace.

Romans 3:23-24 All have sinned and are not good enough for God's glory, and all need to be made right with God by his grace, which is a free gift. They need to be made free from sin through Jesus Christ.

Ephesians 1:7-9 In Christ we are set free by the blood of his death, and so we have forgiveness of sins. How rich is God's grace, which he has given to us so fully and freely. God, with full wisdom and understanding, let us know his secret purpose. This was what God wanted, and he planned to do it through Christ.

2 Timothy 2:1 You then, Timothy, my child, be strong in the grace we have in Christ Jesus.

Titus 3:6-7 God poured out richly upon us that Holy Spirit through Jesus Christ our Savior. Being made right with God by his grace, we could have the hope of receiving the life that never ends.

Marriage

Matthew 19:4-12 Jesus answered, "Surely you have read in the Scriptures: When God made the world, 'he made them male and female.' And God said, 'So a man will leave his father and mother and be united with his wife, and the two will become one body.' So there are not two, but one. God has joined the two together, so no one should separate them."

The Pharisees asked, "Why then did Moses give a command for a man to divorce his wife by giving her divorce papers?"

Jesus answered, "Moses allowed you to divorce your wives because you refused to accept God's teaching, but divorce was not allowed in the beginning. I tell you that anyone who divorces his wife and marries another woman is guilty of adultery. The only reason for a man to divorce his wife is if his wife has sexual relations with another man."

The followers said to him, "If that is the only reason a man can divorce his wife, it is better not to marry."

Jesus answered, "Not everyone can accept this teaching, but God has made some able to accept it. There are different reasons why some men cannot marry. Some men were born without the ability to become fathers. Others were made that way later in life by other people. And some men have given up marriage because of the kingdom of heaven. But the person who can marry should accept this teaching about marriage."

Mark 10:10-12 Later, in the house, his followers asked Jesus again about the question of divorce. He answered, "Anyone who divorces his wife and marries another woman is guilty of adultery against her. And the woman who divorces her husband and marries another man is also guilty of adultery."

1 Corinthians 7:1-16 Now I will discuss the things you wrote me about. It is good for a man not to have sexual relations with a woman. But because sexual sin is a danger, each man should have his own wife, and each woman should have her own husband. The husband should give his wife all that he owes her as his wife. And the wife should give her husband all that she owes him as her husband. The wife does not have full rights over her own body; her husband shares them. And the husband does not have full rights over his own body; his wife shares them. Do not refuse to give your bodies to each other, unless you both agree to stay away from sexual relations for a time so you can give your time to prayer. Then come together again so Satan cannot tempt you because of a lack of self-control. I say this to give you permission to stay away from sexual relations for a time. It is not a command to do so. I wish that everyone were like me, but each person has his own gift from God. One has one gift, another has another gift.

Now for those who are not married and for the widows I say this: It is good for them to stay unmarried as I am. But if they cannot control themselves, they should marry. It is better to marry than to burn with sexual desire.

Now I give this command for the married people. (The command is not from me; it is from the Lord.) A wife should not leave her husband. But if she does leave, she must not marry again, or she should make up with her husband. Also the husband should not divorce his wife.

For all the others I say this (I am saying this, not the Lord): If a Christian man has a wife who is not a believer, and she is happy to live with him, he must not divorce her. And if a Christian woman has a husband who is not a believer, and he is happy to live with her, she must not divorce him. The husband who is not a believer is made holy through his believing wife. And the wife who is not a believer is made holy through her believing husband. If this were not true, your children would not be clean, but now your children are holy.

But if those who are not believers decide to leave, let them leave. When this happens, the Christian man or woman is free. But God called us to live in peace. Wife, you don't know; maybe you will save your husband. And husband, you don't know; maybe you will save your wife.

1 Corinthians 7:39 A woman must stay with her husband as long as he lives. But if her husband dies, she is free to marry any man she wants, but she must marry in the Lord.

1 Corinthians 6:13-20 "Food is for the stomach, and the stomach for food," but God will destroy them both. The body is not for sexual sin but for the Lord, and the Lord is for the body. By his power God has raised the Lord from the dead and will also raise us from the dead. Surely you know that your bodies are parts of Christ himself. So I must never take the parts of Christ and join them to a prostitute! It is written in the Scriptures, "The two will become one body." So you should know that anyone who joins with a prostitute becomes one body with the prostitute. But the one who joins with the Lord is one spirit with the Lord.

So run away from sexual sin. Every other sin people do is outside their bodies, but those who sin sexually sin against their own bodies. You should know that your body is a temple for the Holy Spirit who is in you. You have received the Holy Spirit from God. So you do not belong to yourselves, because you were bought by God for a price. So honor God with your bodies.

Hebrews 13:4 Marriage should be honored by everyone, and husband and wife should keep their marriage pure. God will judge as guilty those who take part in sexual sins.

Colossians 3:18-19 Wives, yield to the authority of your husbands, because this is the right thing to do in the Lord.

Husbands, love your wives and be gently with them.

Romans 7:1-3 Brothers and sisters, all of you understand the law of Moses. So surely you know that the law rules over people only while they are alive. For example, a woman must stay married to her husband as long as he is alive. But if her husband dies, she is free from the law of marriage. But if she marries another man while her husband is still alive, the law says she is guilty of adultery. But if her husband dies, she is free from the law of marriage. Then if she marries another man, she is not guilty of adultery.

Ephesians 5:21-33 Yield to obey each other because you respect Christ.

Wives, yield to your husbands, as you do to the Lord, because the husband is the head of the wife, as Christ is the head of the church. And he is the Savior of the body, which is the church. As the church yields to Christ, so you wives should yield to your husbands in everything.

Husbands, love your wives as Christ loved the church and gave himself for it to make it belong to God. Christ used the word to make the church clean by washing it with water. He died so that he could give the church to himself like a bride in all her beauty. He died so that the church could be pure and without fault, with no evil or sin or any other wrong thing in it. In the same way, husbands should love their wives as they love their own bodies. The man who loves his wife loves himself. No one ever hates his own body, but feeds and takes care of it. And that is what Christ does for the church, because we are parts of his body. The Scripture says, "So a man will leave his father and mother and be united with his wife, and the two will become one body." That secret is very important—I am talking about Christ and the church. But each one of you must love his wife as he loves himself, and a wife must respect her husband.

About the Author

Thomas Sutton graduated from San Jose State University with a degree in Environmental Studies Urban and Regional Planning. He has published several other books including *2199, Jesus the Christ*, and *Zommer II*. He is currently working on his next book.

www.ingramcontent.com/pod-product-compliance
Lightning Source LLC
Chambersburg PA
CBHW030304290526
45785CB00001B/203